TURN OF FATE

TURN OF FATE

HOW ONE WOMAN'S
JOURNEY OF SURVIVAL
LED HER TO FIND
TRUE PURPOSE

MELISSA AYRES

I have tried to recreate events, locales and conversations from my memories of
them. In order to maintain their anonymity in some instances I have changed
the names of individuals and places, I may have changed some identifying
characteristics and details such as physical properties, occupations and places
of residence.

I dedicate this book to my parents,
Harold & Miyoko Underwood, who have always
been there for me, and to the man who believed in me
and changed my life with his love, Bruce Ayres

I sit on the beach in front of our house in Hawaii, watching the sunrise, remembering all of the beautiful moments my husband and I shared over the almost twenty years we were together. Memories of a man I loved more than life itself fill my mind. Time will pass as I continue my journey without him. I can hear his voice telling me how much he loved me; telling me that he couldn't imagine his life without me. I feel the same about him—only I don't have to imagine it, because it is now my reality.

CHAPTER ONE

One of my earliest childhood memories is questioning why, and how, I was still here on this earth. At a very young age, I found myself wondering: what is my real purpose? For surely, given the seemingly random events that I had lived through, there must have been some deeper purpose—if only I could uncover it.

Of course, some would say that none of it was random—that what happened to me, or indeed what happens to any of us, is not by chance.

My journey started long before I was born, in a distant country. My father, Harry, was in the Navy, stationed at a base in Yokosuka, Japan. There, in the spring of 1956, he met the woman he was going to marry. My mother, Miyoko, had just moved to Yokosuka from her hometown, Sasebo, more than 700 miles away. Her sister, Tomiko, had recently married an American merchant seaman and had gone to live in Yokosuka so she could be there when his ship came in. Her husband would be gone for extended periods of time, and Tomiko wasn't fond of living alone, so she asked my mother to go stay with her.

The girlfriend of one of my father's shipmates introduced my parents. On their first date, he took her to the officers' club for dinner and tried to impress her by ordering filet mignon for the both of them. When the steaks arrived, my mother appeared puzzled as to what to do next. My father, noticing her distress, cut the steak for her. He later discovered that, in Japan, food is always cut in bite-size pieces before it's served, so it was very surprising to her to have this big slab of meat just sitting on the plate.

My mother hardly spoke a word of English, and my father had learned only a few words in Japanese, so whenever my dad told me this story as a child, I would think: What do you do on a date when someone doesn't speak the same language as you? Do you just stare at one another the entire evening? The language barrier didn't matter to my father, who says that he knew on their second date they would be together for life. He left for sea the following morning and upon returning, searched for my mother immediately after pulling into port. My aunt was leaving in a few weeks to live in New York, so my parents rented a small house in Ohtsu, a suburb outside of Yokosuka, and moved in together.

My mother, the daughter of a construction contractor, was the third youngest of thirteen children. Her mother had died when she was eleven, and her father was left to raise the children on his own. She was born in the 1930s, when times were hard, so the children all had to pitch in to run the household, the oldest having to take care of the youngest.

My father had a very modest upbringing, growing up in Lexington, Kentucky, the son of a shoemaker and the oldest of three children. He had been a wiry boy, an introvert who had very little self-confidence, and because of that he received poor grades. After he graduated from high school, a neighbor who was working at American Optical lined up a job for him. When he enlisted in the Navy and they asked him what he did in civilian life, he said "optician," so they sent him to optical school. Because it was something that interested him, he excelled, finishing second in his class.

About three months after my parents moved in together, my father asked my mother to marry him, and then immediately began filling out the paperwork, seeking the Navy's approval for the marriage. In 1956 there was still a lot of prejudice against the Japanese, interracial marriages were frowned upon, and it was hard for military personnel to get permission to marry a foreign national. Believing my mother was worth fighting for, he relentlessly pursued his superiors and three months later was given permission to marry.

They wed at the Tokyo embassy in November of 1956. So my mother could acclimate to living in America someday, they moved into base housing, and my father enrolled her in a bridal school. The aim of the school, which was run by the officers' wives, was to teach the Japanese brides of Navy personnel what they would experience living in America—in essence, teaching them the American way. My mother was taught how to use a vacuum cleaner, and make homemade apple pie and spaghetti. As the Italian cook instructed the class in how to boil pasta, my mother watched intently and was quite shocked when the instructor threw a noodle up to the ceiling and informed the class that if it stuck, it was done. My mother thought that was the craziest thing ever. I'm sure she questioned what kind of country she was preparing to move to. Yet she was determined to learn how to cook this thing called "spaghetti," and she did. She would make it for us when we were growing up, and it continues to be one of her favorites today.

When my parents spent their first Thanksgiving together, they wanted it to be special, so they decided to make dinner and invite all of their friends. Only there was one big problem: neither of them knew how to cook a turkey. Needless to say, it was a complete disaster. When the frozen turkey was taken out of the oven and they discovered it had not cooked, they decided to leave it in the oven for another three to four hours until it finally cooked through. I'm sure there was a lot of alcohol that got passed around the table that evening until the feast was ready to be served.

Two years later, my father was transferred to the Navy Department in Washington, D.C. On the way there, they scheduled a stop in his hometown, Lexington, Kentucky, so he could introduce his new wife to the family. My father was a bit concerned his family might not be accepting of my mom—after all, many people in the United States still held a lot of animosity toward the Japanese from the war. My mother wasn't concerned, and by now she had learned enough English to be able to hold a conversation when she met my dad's family.

They had an epic journey to get to the United States. First they boarded a US naval ship to Yokohama for an eleven-day trip to Seattle. From there they flew on the Pan Am Constellation to Chicago, where they transferred to a DC3 to Lexington, Kentucky. During one of their flights, they were served champagne, and as my mother took her first sip, she looked at my father and said, "Do people actually pay for this?" My father could only laugh. He was a simple man, and he probably thought the same. I believe she never tried alcohol again after that day. Growing up, we used to joke that she could get drunk by smelling the lid of a beer can, and it would make her madder than hell.

My father's family was respectful and treated my mother with kindness, but my father could tell his mother had some pent-up resentment toward her because of the war; she wasn't quite ready to forgive the Japanese. For as long as she lived, my grandmother never fully accepted my mother, who was very aware of her mother-in-law's hostility toward her. If my mother walked into the kitchen to lend a hand, my grandmother would snub her and tell her she didn't need her help.

In Washington, D.C., my mother settled into her new life with great ease. She improved her English by watching old movies on television. Every day when my father returned home from work, she would have written down a list of words, and she would ask him the meaning of them. In a very short period of time, she was speaking English fluently.

It always seems to be the simple moments that touch our lives and that we remember the best: as a kid, I remember coming inside after playing on a Saturday afternoon, and she would be watching old John Wayne movies on TV or listening to Simon and Garfunkel on the record player. Her favorite song, and mine, too, was "Bridge Over Troubled Water."

In 1962, my father received orders to attend Field Medicine School in Camp Pendleton, California, and then go on to the First Marine Brigade in Kaneohe, Hawaii. Mom and Dad set out in their new Pontiac Bonneville convertible to drive across the country to San Francisco, where they would fly to Hawaii. The day they left Washington, D.C., was an important one for my mother for another reason: it was the day she received her U.S. citizenship papers.

While stopping over in Kentucky to visit my father's family on the way to California, my father learned that the Navy had changed his transfer papers and were no longer sending him to Hawaii after his training. "Looks like you're off to Cuba, son," my grandfather joked. Tensions were running high all around the country at the time, as President John F. Kennedy had just put the Cuban blockade in place. That same day, my father received a call from Washington, D.C., informing him that they were once again changing his orders: a good friend and schoolmate of his had put in a good word, and they were now transferring him to Pearl Harbor, Hawaii.

That day represented so much to my parents. Less than two decades before, the United States had been at war with my mother's country, and now, having just obtained her U.S. citizenship, she would be living in the very place where the Japanese had launched the surprise attack that drew the United States into the war. What a testament to the resilience of humanity.

My parents had been living in Hawaii for only three days when they were awoken at 1:00 AM by sirens and the sound of planes taking off. Thinking they were under attack, they turned on the radio and learned that the island was going to be hit by catastrophic tidal waves at any moment, and anyone who was living in low-lying areas needed to move to higher ground immediately. Still dressed in their pajamas, they raced to the car—and soon realized that every street was downhill from their house. They turned around and went back inside. The realization hit them of just how lucky they were to live on a hill when they heard on the radio that the tsunami, while only a one-foot wave, had traveled at 600 miles per hour, causing considerable damage near the shore.

One of Dad's acquaintances was Hawaiian senator Daniel Inouye, whom he had met back in Washington, D.C. Dad had become friends with the owner of a Japanese market in a bad part of D.C. All the Japanese nationals frequented the store, including Senator Inouye when he was in town, and the storeowner had introduced them to each other. When President Kennedy came to Hawaii to meet with the senator, Dad was determined

 to commemorate the visit with a photo of the two men together. When their motorcade passed by, my father grabbed his camera. There they were, stopped at a traffic light, sitting in a convertible with the top down. President Kennedy saw my father, who had fitted him with sunglasses at the White House, and stood up in the car and waved. That photo was taken in June of 1963, just five months before Kennedy's assassination. All through my childhood, the photo hung on the wall in my father's office.

For years my parents had tried to have children, and while they were living in Hawaii, my mother's doctor told them she would never be able to conceive. They wanted to have a family, and they weren't going to allow the doctor's news to deter them. They immediately located a local adoption agency and filed papers to adopt my eldest brother, Howard. His adoption was finalized on September 23rd, my father's birthday. A year passed, and they made the decision to adopt my sister, Suzie. Once again, the date the adoption was finalized fell on my father's birthday. My father even asked the adoption agency if they had planned it so the adoptions came through on his birthday, and they assured him that it was just a coincidence.

Once they had a family, my mother and father were happier than they had ever been.

But then, just a few months after my sister's adoption, the family was split up because my father was shipped off to Vietnam. Three months into his service there, he would get ten days of R&R in Yokosuka. My parents were so determined for the family to be together that a month before his R&R, my mother traveled all the way to Japan by ship with Howard and Suzie—who were both younger than two years old at the time—so they could be there to meet my dad at the port when his ship came in. After his ten-day leave ended, my father returned to Vietnam, and my mother, brother, and sister got back on a ship to Hawaii.

Fortunately, the family was reunited in Washington, D.C., when my father was transferred back to the Navy Department after only a short stint in Vietnam. My father's commanding officer, Dr. George Burkley, had been appointed White House physician, and my father became the White House optician.

One day, President Johnson informed my father that he wanted a pair of glasses "just like Bob's." My father didn't know who Bob was but answered, "Yes, Mr. President." When he left the Oval Office, he asked the Secret Service agent stationed by the door, "Who the hell is Bob?" It turned out the President meant Bob McNamara, the Secretary of Defense. So my father ordered a car to take him to the Pentagon so he could see Bob's glasses.

I'm amazed my father can still remember the name of the style all these years later: Shuron Shurset Rimway rimless glasses.

My father was informed by the White House staff to make seven pairs, one for the President and one for each of the President's aides. He went back to his office and had seven pairs made, only with a slight modification: they had to dull the gold on the frames to reduce glare during television appearances.

When my father arrived at the White House to deliver the glasses, President Johnson said in a rude tone, "That's not what I want." My father informed the President that the frames were exactly like Bob's. President Johnson proceeded to describe the frames he wanted, and my father soon realized that the type of glasses the President wanted were nothing like Bob McNamara's glasses; what he really wanted was a French-made semi-rimless frame. So back to the office my father went to start the process all over again. He finished the order and returned to deliver them, and thankfully that time the President was satisfied.

My father was called to the White House early one morning to adjust the glasses he had made for President Johnson. He joined a party of about half a dozen men, including two Navy captains, waiting to see the President. They were all escorted into the President's bedroom, and there he stood—buck naked. When my father tells this story, he always adds, "And it wasn't a pretty sight." They all stood and patiently watched while the President dressed. He was wrapped in some sort of elastic corset to pull in his stomach, and, as usual, he wasn't in a good mood. The President chewed out one of his staff members and then ripped his steward a new one because his zipper was stuck. Then, for some reason, in a very nasty voice the President shouted, "Shut up—I don't want to hear that now." It was my father's turn next, and he was happy to finish adjusting the President's glasses and get back to his office. He wondered why the President had chosen such a delicate eyeglass frame, knowing my father would have to be called often to adjust them.

Dr. Burkley would tell my father, "Don't screw this up, or you will be shipped back to Vietnam." My father would laugh, but he took what the doctor said seriously and was very careful about every move he made while in the White House. He outlasted Johnson, and during the Nixon administration, he would be called on to fit glasses for the President and his daughter, Julie Nixon Eisenhower, and for Vice President Agnew's family.

My brother and sister began campaigning for another sister and relentlessly pursued my parents until they told the adoption agency they wished to adopt again. Not long after, the agency told them about a baby girl who had been born on Christmas Day at the Malcolm Grow medical facility on Andrews Air Force Base in Maryland. My adoption was soon finalized, and I was taken to my new home to meet my brother and sister.

Just when it seemed my parents had the family they always wanted, it came under jeopardy. It was the spring of 1970, and my father returned home from work one day to news from my mother that I was running a fever. They took me to the Navy Department medical clinic, where a doctor examined me but was unable to pinpoint the cause of my fever. He said he did not want to start me on antibiotics without a diagnosis, so he made an appointment for me to return the next day and told my parents to bring me back sooner if my fever worsened.

The next morning, my fever seemed stable, so my father left early for work in order to beat the traffic. Just after he left, my mother retook my temperature—suddenly it had reached more than 106 degrees. I began having a grand mal seizure, losing consciousness and going into convulsions. She picked me up and rushed me next door to the neighbor, who immediately called 911. On the way to the hospital, I stopped breathing and had to be resuscitated.

In the emergency room, they quickly administered Valium, which succeeded in bringing down my fever, but it was apparent there was something seriously wrong. When my father arrived at the hospital, he decided against admitting me there and had me transported to the hospital on Andrews Air Force Base in Maryland—the very same place I had been born just three months earlier. After running numerous tests, a pediatrician performed a spinal tap, which came back positive for pneumococcal meningitis, a bacterial infection that causes inflammation of the membranes around the brain.

Back then, most babies with pneumococcal meningitis didn't fare well. The doctor gave my parents an overly optimistic fifty-fifty chance of my survival, but they knew it was much less. I was admitted and placed on antibiotics through an IV drip.

The doctor's instincts had been correct. The antibiotics worked and his quick thinking saved my life that day; I was one of the lucky ones. I remained on IV antibiotics twenty-four hours a day for almost a month before I was well enough to go home and live my life. Most babies who survived this form of meningitis were left with brain damage, seizures, hearing loss, or paralysis. It could take time for the damage to become apparent, and because my temperature had remained very high for a long time before I started receiving antibiotics, the doctor wasn't quite sure what the outcome would be for me.

CHAPTER TWO

I grew up in a small town on the water in Maryland, just minutes from Washington, D.C. I had a great childhood, though I didn't realize just how lucky I was until I was an adult. It was a very wholesome upbringing; some would say it was very "Leave it to Beaver." It was a time when we didn't have to lock our doors, and we knew all of our neighbors. We were never bored, because to us playing with friends and being creative was exciting. We kept busy making up games and doing things kids today would find dull, like smashing inkberries in a Frisbee and using them to write on the sidewalk. We would ride our bikes for miles without our parents having a concern. There were no cell phones back then, and even if they had existed, we wouldn't have needed them—we preferred using old soup cans with strings attached, anyway.

When I was four years old, our family was completed by the addition of another brother—only this time, my parents didn't have to make a trip to the adoption agency. My mother had discovered that she was pregnant. What a surprise it was for my parents to realize that it was possible for them to conceive after all. My brother Russel was born in August 1973, and, with the exception of being shaped like a cucumber, he was a healthy baby boy. As he grew, I became closer to Russel than my other siblings, and we did everything together. I would lead him into my parent's room and, careful not to get caught, go into my mother's closet and pull out her dresses and heels and

make him wear them— we would both laugh for hours. He was very intelligent, and he had a gentle soul, much like my father's.

I can't remember a time during my childhood when my parents weren't there for me and my sister and brothers. They would get up early to make us breakfast, and lunch for school. When we woke up, lined up on the kitchen counter, there were slices of Wonder Bread, and we had our choice of peanut butter and jelly, or ham and cheese. Into each of our lunchboxes they would place a Thermos filled with cherry Kool-Aid, a bag of Fritos or Cheetos, and a piece of fruit. I always went for the ham and cheese, and Cheetos, while my brothers and sister opted for the peanut butter and jelly, and Fritos. (I was always the rebel in the family!) If we were running late for school, we would usually be handed Pop-Tarts wrapped in napkins as we ran out the door, and we'd eat them on the bus.

When we got home from school, we'd run into the kitchen, where my mother would be waiting. We would throw our lunchboxes on the counter, and as Mom opened them to clean them, she would usually find that the fruit was still there. (Fruit was a lousy commodity for trade at lunchtime.) Mom would give us a snack, and we'd do our homework and go outside to play. Dinner was always at 6:30 PM. Afterward, we were allowed to go back outside until the street lights came on, and then we would all watch television until it was time for bed. We would brush our teeth and go to our bedrooms, and usually about five minutes after everything was quiet, one of us would walk into the kitchen to get a drink, complaining we were thirsty. We made up every excuse in the book not to have to go to bed.

My father taught me everything he could about kindness and what I needed to succeed in the world. He retired from the Navy in 1971 to work as an optician, and he would take me to hang out with him at his office. I would sit and watch as patients tried on glasses, and they would ask me which ones looked best. I was just a kid, but I certainly always gave my opinion. If I got tired, I'd go back in the corner and lie on a chair to take a nap. I guess none of the patients minded because I was little and cute at the time. Besides, my father has never been overly concerned about what others think; he has always lived his life with a simple kindness.

I was eight years old when I began going to Dad's office every Saturday so I could earn extra money by cleaning, and filing the patient cards. He would pay me ten dollars, which was probably a lot at that time for an eight-year-old. On our way home, we would stop by the bank so I could deposit the money I had earned, and the ladies who worked there found it cute that I was making money and already had a checking account at my age. I was pretty thrifty and rarely spent a dime, learning a habit that would be beneficial for me in the years to come.

One Saturday, I met one of my father's patients, Mrs. Huntley. She said she was suffering from emphysema, and she seemed very old and frail to me, although later I found out she was only in her sixties. When she left the office, my father explained to me what emphysema was and told me that Mrs. Huntley didn't have much family to care for her. When she came back for her glasses, we sat and talked while she was waiting. She invited me to her house for tea, and there our friendship began.

Every Saturday after I finished filing, my father would drive me to Mrs. Huntley's house, which was just down the street from his office. I would clean her house, because the dust made it hard for her to breathe, she would make me tea, and we would sit and talk until my father came to get me. She would always try to pay me, but I refused because I didn't feel right taking money from her. Besides, I liked spending time with her. She shared stories about her childhood, and I could see it made her happy to remember a simpler time in her life; it made me feel good to know she wasn't alone. I did this every weekend for the next four years, until I became boy crazy and stopped going to see her. Not too long after, I heard she had died. I felt guilty, thinking that if I had continued to visit her, she might still be alive.

My father had a girl working for him at his optometry practice, Christine, and she and her family were to become a big part of my life. Dad would joke that Christine, a pretty Italian girl, was great for business, because all the male customers suddenly needed their glasses adjusted more often. She came from a very close traditional Italian family who were as kind as the day is long. They accepted me as if I were one of their own. I spent hours at their home, cooking with them in the kitchen. After all, they were Italian, so food was family.

Christine has remained in my life, through even the hardest times. What I remember most about her back then is how she treated everyone with kindness. Whether you were a stranger or someone she knew well, it didn't matter. My parents were the same, and as I look back today, I appreciate just how lucky I was to have the role models I did when I was growing up. I was blessed to have not just one loving family, but two.

☆   ☆   ☆

One of the greatest dilemmas for us as children was who was going to get up and change the television channel—there were six to choose from. My sister, Suzie, would pay my little brother, Russel, ten cents to do it. Ten cents back then was a lot to us kids; it bought you five pieces of candy from the local mini-mart. The man behind the register would count the pieces out one at a time and place them in a paper bag. We did everything we could as kids to earn money, and we had pride when we saw our piggy bank grow. I look back now and think Russel could have asked for more, and Suzie probably would have paid it.

When I tell kids about Suzie's arrangement with Russel, all they can say is, "I can't believe there were only six television channels."

The summer would come, school would let out, and we didn't have a care in the world. In the evening, we would catch lightning bugs—or fireflies, depending on where you grew up—and put them in a jar. For some reason, it always seemed to be an old pickle jar. We would put a leaf at the bottom, poke holes in the lid with an ice pick, place it on the nightstand, and watch the fireflies light up all night. The next morning, we would let them go and start the process all over again. We spent our days playing hopscotch in the streets, and jump rope and jacks on the sidewalk.

It was a special treat when my older brother, Howard, and his friends let my friend Pari and I hang out with them in the fort they had built in the woods. They had dug a hole and built a small structure, complete with windows and a tunnel for the entrance. I was surprised they invited us, because Howard had told me that they didn't like girls and we would never be allowed in their fort. Maybe they thought we were different compared to the other girls—or perhaps I had something on Howard at the time that could get him in trouble, and he was playing it safe.

Not too far from their fort was a pond where we would catch tadpoles and go back every day to watch them gradually turn into frogs. One afternoon, Howard lifted a flattened aluminum trashcan lid that was lying by the edge of the pond, and under it were three coiled-up snakes. One opened its jaws to display its fangs and the inside of its mouth, which was a shock of white. It was a water moccasin—now I could see why they were also called "cottonmouths." As the snake began to slither toward us, we all ran—but I don't think we really knew just how poisonous they were, or we would have been more afraid.

Most of the summer, we lived in our pool, playing games such as Marco Polo, which was like tag, and my favorite, Hot Foot, in which we would all jump in the pool, someone would yell "hot foot," and we would all go running to the hot street. During summers back east, the days were in the high nineties, they were humid, and the streets were steaming hot. Whoever could stand in the same place on the street without moving the longest would win. The heat would eventually dry up the puddles that had been cooling our feet, and that is when it got tough. I look back now and think, "What did we win? Blisters?"

Then there were the countless games of Monopoly that usually ended in the board and pieces going flying in the air and someone yelling, "He/she cheated!" In the basement was a TV room we called the "wreck room" because that is usually what it was after we'd been in there. There was red shag carpet and brown wood paneling—well, it was the seventies, you know. Howard would get down on the floor, and we would climb from one piece of furniture to the next as he reached up to try and pull us down. We called that game "Lava Monster," and it usually ended in a big fight and Howard chasing me up the stairs as I ran for my life, screaming to my mom, "Help, he is trying to kill me!" My mom would yell, "Ignore him." And to think, I actually survived!

During the summer, I would go to Jacksonville, Florida, to visit my aunt Tomiko, my mother's sister, and Uncle Alfred, her husband. The tradition started when I was barely four and my brother Russel had just been born. Because he had replaced me as the youngest, he had begun getting all the attention, and I didn't like it. Seeing how the jealousy was affecting me, my parents sent me to stay with my aunt for the rest of that summer. I took my first solo flight, and I remember every detail as if it were yesterday. I was flying Eastern Air Lines, and as the plane began to board, my parents each gave me a big hug and handed me off to an airline stewardess. She walked me to my seat, which was the first aisle seat in the plane, and pinned an Eastern badge to my dress. Throughout the flight she came back to check on me, but I wasn't afraid for a moment—I was going on an adventure!

The day I arrived in Florida, Aunt Tomiko introduced me to the next-door neighbors' three daughters—Maribel, Anna Marie, and Theresa—who were close to me in age. From that moment on, we were inseparable. Three sons of a friend of my aunt's—Michael, Mark, and Matt—along with Michelle, the daughter of another of my aunt's friends, also became part of our gang. I would go on to spend part of the summer at my aunt's for the next ten years, and we all built a bond that would last a lifetime.

Maribel, Anna Marie, and Theresa would throw rocks at my window, which was on the second floor, to get my attention to come out and play, or I would open the window and yell for them to rescue me from my aunt when I was in trouble, which was often. She was strict—you didn't get away with anything in her house—but we knew it came from love. Aunt Tomiko never had children of her own, so I believe that in a way we were her surrogate children. She was constantly entertaining us, and she enjoyed every minute of it. She would load us all into the car, and we would go to either the beach or the base swimming pool. At night we would spray ourselves down with bug spray and would all pile into her car—I can still remember the scent of the chemicals—and head to the ball field to watch one of the boys play in a little league game.

It was a simpler and kinder time in America then. We were taught to respect our elders and ourselves, work hard, and gain pride from a job well done. Our parents would do whatever they could to make a better life for their children, and they believed in the American Dream. It was a time that I feel fortunate to have been raised in, a time that set me up with what I needed to live a good life, no matter what happens in my life.

It was a time when sisters and brothers were forced to figure out how to get along—no one was stepping in to do it for us. Little did we know, we were learning a valuable skill that would help us when we grew up. When kids asked Mom or Dad how to spell a word, the reply was always, "Go look it up in the dictionary." The response was usually "How am I going to be able to look it up if I can't spell it?" But somehow we figured it out, and life went on.

Looking back on my childhood on the outskirts of D.C., I see where my sense of patriotism comes from. It truly was such a wholesome time in America. Some would say it was the end of the age of innocence. So much has changed, and I'm not sure that it's been for the better. If given the opportunity, I would like to go back to that simpler time in life.

CHAPTER THREE

I t seemed that, unlike so many other children who survived pneumococcal meningitis, I did not have lasting damage from the illness I'd had as a baby. Yet my parents had been taking me to see doctors since I was two years old. That was when I began running to my mother in a distressed state, telling her, "Someone is chasing me!" She would sit on the floor and hold me until my fear passed. I would then go back to playing, as if nothing had ever happened.

To soothe me, my mother would play records after my dad left for work in the morning. The very first song I remember listening to was "Take Me Home, Country Roads" by John Denver. Mom would play that album for me as I sat next to the stereo speaker, and I would cry when the record ended, which was her cue to turn it over. She must have been so sick of hearing John Denver day in and day out. I found peace in music, and when I was having a tough time as a child, it was the only thing that seemed to help. It is still my greatest escape today.

These attacks of fear were the first sign of what my parents and I would later call my "episodes." When I had an episode, I would stare blankly. Although I could hear what was going on around me, I couldn't make out what people were saying. If I was holding something, I would drop it.

I saw countless doctors and had almost every test run on me. As I look back now as an adult, I feel very lucky to have been adopted by parents who loved me as if I were their own birth child and who were relentless in trying to find a diagnosis for me and weren't going to give up until they did. The doctors would tell my parents that I had a heart murmur and that it was nothing to worry about, as I would outgrow it. But by the time I was in elementary school, I knew there was more to it than that. There was something wrong with me.

I had an episode during track and field one day, but I struggled through the race and continued to the finish line and came in second. I was determined not to allow anything to stand in my way of doing what I wanted and living my life. Even though I sensed there was something wrong with me, I had programmed myself at a very young age to live life as if I were normal, as if I were no different from everyone else.

One winter's evening when I was twelve years old, with a fire roaring in the hearth, my father sat on the sofa reading a book while I played my favorite albums on the record player, which sat on a shelf next to the fireplace. (Now that I think about it, it probably wasn't the greatest place to store records.) I started to have an episode and went to sit down next to Dad until it passed. After it ended, I realized the episodes were getting worse. I said to my father, "Before I die, I want to make a difference in this world."

In the next few years, the symptoms got worse. I began vomiting each time I had an episode, sometimes as often as five times a day. In a year, this progressed to losing control of my bladder when I had an episode, which made it difficult at school.

When I was fourteen, we went to see a new doctor at the hospital, who referred me to a neurologist in Bethesda, Maryland, where the President of the United States goes for medical care. I began explaining my symptoms, and within ten minutes she was able to diagnose me with complex partial seizures. I didn't care what I had—I was just grateful that someone finally knew what was wrong with me.

The neurologist scheduled numerous tests, including one using a new machine that had just been acquired by the hospital. When I arrived for my appointment, I was told I was one of the first patients to have an MRI at their facility. I thought, "What in the heck is an MRI?" I was led outside to a trailer, where the test was to be performed, because back then hospitals weren't equipped to have MRI machines indoors. The technician was reading a manual. "Are you sure you know how to work this thing?" I asked him.

"Are you sure you don't have any metal on?" he asked me.

"Why?" I eventually asked, having already assured him several times that I didn't.

He replied, "If you do, you'll get stuck to the machine, and we'll have to call someone to come and take apart the machine to get you out."

Looking down at the cotton surgical gown I was wearing, I said, "Nope, no metal. We're good. Let's get this thing over with."

The technician strapped a helmet on my head and rolled me into the machine—it was dark and very cramped. It was a good thing I wasn't claustrophobic, or I would have been in big trouble, because I was in there for almost two hours. He didn't give me earplugs or headphones, as they do now when you have an MRI. I lay in the dark, with a slight breeze from a fan cooling my skin, listening to what sounded like the loudest jackhammer right in my ears. The technician would come in every twenty minutes or so to ask how I was doing, and the answer was always the same: bored. When the scan ended, I was glad to get out of that machine and get back to school.

This was more than thirty years ago, and back then it took a week or longer for the doctor to receive the test results. Finally, the news came: my seizures were being caused by a brain tumor. It was not cancer, but it was considered inoperable. My only option was to take seizure medication, and I was prescribed Tegretol. I could feel the change almost immediately: the medication had terrible side effects. I felt very agitated and didn't feel like myself, and some days I was very tired. I had to have my blood tested frequently, because it could affect my white cell counts.

The doctors never seemed to be able to get the levels of the medication correct. My seizures would come under control, and then they would worsen again, so I had to figure out ways to adapt. School was sometimes challenging. While reading a book in class, I would have a seizure and forget what I had just read and have to read it all over again. It was very frustrating, but somehow I was able to get good grades.

No one except my immediate family knew that I had a brain tumor and seizures. Life was hard enough just being a kid. I thought if the other kids knew I had seizures, I would be relentlessly teased, so I learned how to disguise my seizures when I had them in class. I would pretend I was tired and confused. Sometimes, a seizure would be worse than others, and I would have a harder time covering it up.

One day stands out in my mind. I was sitting in my high school English class and had a pretty bad seizure that went on for longer than usual. After it was over, the boy sitting next to me asked, "Did you just have a seizure?" I was in shock that he suspected the truth. Maybe he had seizures, too, and none of us knew. Anxious to keep my seizures a secret, I said, "No" and made up an excuse. I'm not sure if he believed me.

Another time in high school, I had a seizure at the end of the day, when school let out. I was standing in front of my locker. I shut the door and attempted to walk to the bus, but I had forgotten how to get out of the school. Intensely afraid and confused, I began to cry. All I wanted at that moment was to feel okay again and get to my bus.

When I was finally able to find my way outside to the front of the building, the bus had already left. Panicking about how I would get home, I walked to the parking lot, hoping I might recognize someone. A boy named Gene, who lived the next street over from me, was there, so I asked him for a ride. I remember the relief I felt when he said "Yes." Little did he know how much it meant to me that day. When you are going through hard times, it can be the simplest act of kindness that makes all the difference.

There was this one kid—every school has this kid—who relentlessly teased me almost every day on the bus, from kindergarten right up until high school, when I could drive. He didn't know that the stress of his bullying would cause me to have more seizures. I would complain to my parents, and they would tell me to ignore him. I resolved that no matter how mean he was to me, I was going to treat him only with kindness. As an adult, I heard that he didn't have an easy childhood, and I was glad that I had been nice to him. Maybe I showed him that someone cared and deep down it meant something to him. Years later I ran into him, and I didn't share with him how hard he had made it for me when I was a kid—it wasn't necessary. I was just happy to see that he had a good life as an adult.

My parents were careful not to make a big deal of my seizures, and I believe that may have changed the course of my life. It taught me to never feel I had any limitations. If they had handled things differently, I may not be the person I am today or have the life I do.

☆   ☆   ☆

At the age of fourteen, I was given the opportunity to work in the lab at a medical center not far from my high school, thanks to a family friend who worked there. I checked in blood donors as they arrived and helped with blood drives offsite on the weekends. I had aspired to being a doctor since I was ten, so I was excited to have the opportunity to work in the medical field and learn everything I could. In less than six months, I was getting more involved in the processing of the blood, having learned how to spin down plasma and platelets.

Soon there was an illness that people were dying from, and no one in the medical community knew what it was. It hadn't been given a name yet, only a number. I remember the fear in people's faces, not knowing if they were going to contract this disease. My supervisors saw I was eager to learn about pathology, and they taught me how to test for this new disease. Not long after, it was given a name: HIV/AIDS.

"Do you think they will be able to cure this?" I asked one of the doctors.

"Not in your lifetime," he replied.

"I think they will probably create a drug first that will keep people alive, before there is a cure," I said.

"I don't think so; it's very complicated," he responded.

It has been fascinating for me to see the great advances that medicine has made over the years in treating HIV/AIDS. People are now able to live with a disease that once killed almost everyone who contracted it.

I learned a lot working at the medical-center lab. The people I worked for taught me a deep work ethic and drive, and most of all, their belief in me inspired me to believe that I could do anything I wanted.

It was as if I had a radar for knowing when a new kid had moved into the neighborhood. One day I stood in the front yard, watching the new neighbors across the street move in, wondering if they had kids. Later that day, I saw a girl around my age walk across her lawn, so I hurried over to meet her. She introduced herself as Lori, and from that day on, we spent all of our time together. The hours we spent in her basement curling our hair, putting on makeup, talking about boys and playing pool, listening to every Van Halen album, were priceless. She always seemed to have a smile on her face and was such a positive person.

I knew a lot of people in school, but being popular never mattered to me. I had my close group of friends and kept it pretty low key. The smaller the group of people I hung out with, the less likely it was that someone would figure out I was having seizures.

As it was the 1980s, for my friends and I, getting dressed in the morning was like playing dress-up on a daily basis. We all thought we were Madonna or were reliving a scene out of the movie *Flashdance,* with our cut-off sweatshirts, leg warmers, and heels. I was the preppy girl—Jordache jeans, polo shirt with the collar up, a sweater tied around my neck, and penny loafers.

Then there were the massive amounts of makeup that we wore, and the can after can of Aqua Net that we went through. We were the MTV generation; I remember the day MTV launched and watching the first music video ever played, "Video Killed the Radio Star" by the Buggles.

My sister Suzie was four years older than me, and you know how that is: little sister always wanting to hang out with the big sister, who didn't want to have anything to do with her. No matter how many times I would be thrown out of Suzie's room, I just kept going back. She listened to Molly Hatchet, Lynyrd Skynyrd, and ZZ Top, which was a far cry from what she'd listened to when she was younger. Back then, she was listening to Donny Osmond. All the girls thought he was cute, but I mostly remember his purple socks. Suzie had all of his albums. I think she wanted to get rid of the evidence, because now I have all of her albums.

It was in high school that I met my first real boyfriend. I was fourteen, and Mike was a senior. He was Italian and had thick, curly hair, big dark eyes, and a smile that made *you* want to smile. I couldn't have had a better first boyfriend, because he had a soft kindness about him. He would carry my books to class and was always respectful. He drove thirty minutes each way from his house every day to pick me up, take me to school, and then drive me home after. On the weekends, he would pick me up and drive me to his house, and I would help him with his chores. I have a lot of great memories of him and our time together. One day, we were washing his car, and as I walked around to his side of the car, he dumped the entire bucket of soapy water on my head. I chased him with the hose, spraying him down, laughing. He had no idea what I was going through with my seizures during that time and how healing that laughter was to me.

Right after high school graduation, when I was barely eighteen, I moved into my own place. I reveled in the newfound freedom. I thought I was so grown up back then, realizing only today how little I really knew. We were all so desperate to be older, not knowing that one day we would wish we could be young again.

CHAPTER FOUR

I t was a lot quieter at home for my mom and dad now. Howard had joined the Navy as a diver, and Suzie was busy working as a manager of a local Pizza Hut. My uncle Melvin had gone to live in Saudi Arabia, and I was renting his home in Tysons Corner, Virginia, while working for a temp agency.

That summer, my mother took my brother Russel, who was fourteen, to Florida to visit my aunt Tomiko. A week later, he decided he was bored and flew home to spend time with his friends. I thought my dad might need some help, so I went back home to stay for the weekend.

Russel and one of his friends, Jack, had set up a tent in the backyard so they could camp out that night—but not until they'd had their usual marathon session at the computer. It was 1987, and people were just starting to have computers in their homes. My brother was one of the original computer geeks; he spent countless hours on the computer, usually late into the night.

"Hey, if I fall asleep with my TV on, can you turn it off before you go out to the backyard?" I asked him before I went to bed.

"Sure," he said, before going to the computer.

I woke to a fuzzy TV screen and white noise—it was midnight, and the station had gone off the air. As I got up to turn the television off, I thought, "This is strange."

In the morning, I called out to Russel, but there was no answer. When I went out to check the tent, there was no one there. My father and I both found it odd that Russel's bike was still in the yard, but he was nowhere in sight. We looked everywhere. No sign of Russel or his friend. I walked all over the neighborhood, searching for him, and as I walked back inside the house, I heard the phone ringing. I listened in on the conversation as my father picked up the receiver. It was the fire department, calling to ask if we knew where my brother was.

"No, we've been looking for him all morning," replied my father.

"We received a phone call from the neighbor at the top of the street, concerned someone may be at the bottom of their pool," said the fire chief.

I don't remember thinking anything at that moment. I ran out the door and headed to the top of the street, faster than I had ever run in my life. I flung open the gate, ran to the pool, and dove in. I wanted to prove they were wrong, that it wasn't him.

The water was dirty, and I could barely see anything in front of me. I searched for what seemed like forever, and as I got to the deep end, I found him. I struggled to get him to the surface.

As I did, I saw several firefighters and my father standing by the edge of the pool. First they lifted my brother out, and then me. I tried performing CPR on Russel as he lay on the pool deck, but it was too late. I couldn't save him.

The events of that day will forever be permanently ingrained in my mind. I remember passing all the neighbors on the walk home, and everything feeling surreal, as if I was in a terrible dream. Watching my father call my mother in Florida to tell her what had happened, and hearing her cry on the other end of the phone. My heart breaking for her. My heart breaking for all of us, because I knew at that moment life had forever changed.

My parents' only birth child, the child that doctors had said would never be possible, was gone. And now my parents had to face life without him. We all had to face life without him.

My mother flew home to a house that was in chaos as we tried to make sense of how this had happened. When I found Russel and pulled him to the surface, he was wearing a diving mask that Howard had given him as a gift. Had Russel thought he could breathe underwater with the mask on? But why was he in the pool in the first place? He had always had an aversion to the water and had never wanted to learn how to swim. Whatever the reason was, I knew we would most likely never know the truth. Even if we did, it wouldn't change the fact he was never coming back. The police investigated and ruled his death to be an accident.

The day of the funeral, hundreds of people, ranging from my parents' friends to the kids we all went to school with, came to pay their respects to my little brother and be there for our family. A policeman, who had stopped by to give his condolences to my father, said, "I haven't seen a funeral procession as long as this in my entire career." I knew my parents were loved by many, but that day showed me just how much.

My brother's death didn't make sense to me, and it probably never will. He was smart and kind, and he had his entire life ahead of him. Even today I sometimes wonder what he would have become when he was older.

For months I had a really hard time sleeping. I kept reliving that day over and over in my mind, wishing there was something I could have done to save Russel, thinking that if I had only gone to check why he hadn't turned off my TV that night, he might still be alive.

When I received an invitation later that year to go out to Los Angeles, I didn't really think about it too hard. I was one to just jump on board for the ride and see where it was going to take me, and maybe this was just the kind of change I needed.

My path to Los Angeles had begun during the summer of Russel's death, when my friend Jay—who was a DJ in Ocean City, Maryland—took me to a concert by the surf music legends Jan and Dean. We were standing in the front row, and the band's keyboard player, Gary, sent someone out and asked to meet me. Jay and I went backstage and met the band, and Gary and I became friends. He asked me to come out to California, so there I was at the airport, eighteen years old, getting ready to board a flight to Los Angeles for the first time. I gave my parents one last hug before joining the other passengers boarding the plane. When I reached the gate, I turned back to see tears running down my father's cheeks. It is only now, as an adult, that I fully understand how hard it must have been for him to see his teenage daughter head off on a 3000-mile journey. But I think my father knew deep down that I would be fine. I had been through such serious health problems as a child and the grief of losing my brother, and I was a strong person with a drive and determination to be someone in this world.

When I left Virginia, it was freezing—the winter was just turning to early spring—and after my plane landed in Los Angeles, I stepped outside, and it was sunny and eighty degrees. Needless to say, it wasn't a hard sell. I knew I was home. The city had all the energy that I had missed out on growing up in the D.C. area. I was a bit of an adventurer, and the city gave me the opportunity to explore. There was every convenience I could ever have imagined, right there at my fingertips. It wasn't long before I had flown home, packed up the rest of my things, and returned to Los Angeles to start a new life.

I stayed with Gary for a couple weeks; then I moved to another friend's house in Hollywood until I figured out where I wanted to live in Los Angeles. I hadn't bought a car yet, so I would walk or take a cab everywhere, which made things especially interesting. It was March, and the weather in the city was steaming hot; it had been in the upper nineties for over a week. I walked to the Ralph's grocery store on Sunset Boulevard.

Perhaps the fact that it was also known as Weird Ralph's or Rockin' Ralph's should have given me a hint of what to expect.

Before going in, I stopped off at the ATM on the corner, and as I withdrew cash, a car full of teen boys stopped and asked, "How much?" At first I thought they must be joking or speaking to someone else. I was dressed in polo shorts, a polo shirt, and flip flops—hardly the outfit of someone who was for sale, I thought. As I stood there, it became clear from the looks on their faces that this was no joke.

"First of all, this isn't for sale. And if it was, you couldn't afford it," I said. I grabbed my money and walked into the store, laughing.

As I made my way through the aisles, I came upon an older man in the frozen-food section. The trench coat he was wearing on a day that was as hot as hell should have set off alarm bells to stay clear of him. As I reached for a tub of ice cream, he turned to me, smiled . . . and flashed me! He was wearing nothing—and I mean nothing—but old white tube socks with a red stripe, and dirty Converse high-top tennis shoes. I abandoned my cart, ran to the front of the store, and had security take care of him. As they escorted him out the door, he turned and looked directly at me, grinning from ear to ear.

Where in the hell had I moved?

One evening I received a call from Gary, saying he was playing at a club close to my friend's house in Hollywood and asking if I wanted to join him. I was always up for friends and music. While I was there, I met Gary's friend Rene, and we began dating. We had been seeing each other for only a couple of weeks when he invited me out to Palm Desert for the weekend. A race-car driver, he worked on the side as a roadie, and that weekend he was working a gig with the Beach Boys and wanted me to be there with him. I spent the weekend hanging with the band, having fun, and listening to all the great beach tunes.

I soon found that Rene was also friends with John Stamos, who sometimes toured with the Beach Boys. One evening, Rene picked me up and told me we were going to stop by John's house for a bit. Rene drove race cars, and we sped down Mulholland as fast as he could drive. I loved the thrill of the speed; it was scary and exciting all at the same time. We walked into John's house, where everything was white and modern. Next thing I knew, we were hanging with John in his bedroom; Rene and I were lying on his bed, while John was on his exercise equipment. I can't remember a word of what we talked about that night—all I could think was, "I am lying on John Stamos's bed. How hot is that?"

My relationship with Rene gradually faded away, but I continued speaking to John and would go and meet him on the "Full House" set. What we had was more of a friendship. I think John appreciated that I was different from most people in Hollywood, because I didn't care that he was famous. I just thought he was a really nice guy.

One day on the set I was waiting for him on the sofa in his dressing room as he took a shower. He came out of the bathroom wrapped in a towel, walked over, and sat on the sofa next to me, and as I turned toward him, he planted a very long kiss on my lips. I was surprised. Of course, I thought he was attractive, but I didn't think he felt that way about me. Maybe he was just curious—he had complimented me a few times on my lips. Soon after that, I met someone and began dating him, and I never spoke to John again. But I have memories of a great guy and an amazing kiss.

Thanks to my DJ friend Jay back home, I soon made another friend who would become a very important person to me as I settled into Los Angeles. I had phoned Jay to tell him I had moved. He didn't seem surprised—I think he knew the east coast wasn't for me. When we hung up, he called his friend Charlie Minor, who lived in Los Angeles, and jokingly said he wanted him to take care of me—on the condition that he couldn't date me.

The following day, I received a call from the infamous—or, as he was often referred to, "Good Time"—Charlie, asking me to meet him for lunch at A&M Records. He was Vice President of record promotion, which meant his job was to get radio stations to play the label's songs. He was a legend in the music industry; artists such as Janet Jackson, The Carpenters, Sting, Quincy Jones, Brian Adams, the Police, and many others can thank Charlie for their success today. The ironic part was that he was a rock star in his own right.

I lived close enough to walk to A&M in Hollywood, and as I made my way down Franklin and turned right onto La Brea, as I did most days, I passed by the hookers who always stood there. I had even begun to know a few of them by name. The scenes I saw on the streets were always bizarre to me, coming from a conservative town in the Washington D.C. area, but I found it entertaining and enjoyed all of it.

Charlie wasn't able to leave for lunch, so he had food delivered to his office, and I filled him in on all of my adventures since I'd moved to Los Angeles. He just laughed, because the experiences I'd had were practically constant in his world and didn't seem odd to him at all.

Charlie turned out to be the one person who, whenever I was having a hard time in Los Angeles, could always make my day better with his generosity and care. He would call and invite me out to dinner with "a group of friends," which in Charlie's case usually meant an entourage of twenty or more people. I never knew whom I was going to meet. No matter where he was in in the world, it was the same. He had this way about him that could make every person in the room feel special. Perhaps it came from his southern upbringing—he was from Atlanta, Georgia. He was renowned for the parties he held at his Malibu beach house. You were always guaranteed to see the most beautiful people in Hollywood there, and you would certainly have fun.

On a Sunday evening, I would pick up food from Dan Tana's, a much-loved Italian restaurant on Santa Monica Boulevard, on my way to his house. We would hang out, and knowing that I was a music fanatic, he'd tell me stories about the artists he worked with and the old days in the music industry. It was just a simple time spent with a friend whose life was normally very rushed and chaotic. His friendship and care meant the world to me. He truly was a caring man, and I am so glad I got to know a side of him that few people did.

I would remain friends with Charlie for years, until his life was cut short in March 1995. I had been worried about him for months, because he was being stalked by a girl he had dated a few times. He now had a new girlfriend, and the morning of one of his famous beach parties, he called everyone and cancelled because he wanted to hang out with her instead. I met a friend for brunch, and when I returned home, I turned on the TV. A special news report came on: "Music mogul murdered in Malibu." Somehow I knew it was Charlie before they mentioned his name. The jilted girl had confronted him in his house and shot him point blank. It was such a tragic loss for the music business and for everyone who knew him.

I was glad to know Charlie just because of the friendship we shared. It also happened to mean that I found myself deep in the music scene. It was always a big party. One night we would be out with Sting; the next night it was Bono, Smokey Robinson, or Quincy Jones. Another night, I found myself sitting next to Elton John at his birthday party at Bar One.

"You aren't from Los Angeles, are you?" said Elton.

"No, why do you ask?" I replied.

"Because you are much too nice and real," he said.

It was a huge compliment, but what made me happiest was that it meant I was still me. I hadn't changed to fit into life in Los Angeles.

One night, a group of us were going to dinner, and at the last minute, my friend Sy decided we should all go to Hugh Hefner's house instead, for the Sunday night dinner and movie. At first I was going to decline, thinking it wasn't my deal, but then I decided it would be one of those "been there, done that" moments. The Playboy Mansion was just a few blocks down the street, but since no one walks in LA, we drove. Greeting us as we walked in were Tony Curtis and Fred Dryer.

When we sat down for dinner, I looked over to see who had sat down next to me, and it was Tony Curtis. We had a nice conversation, and as we were all being escorted into the viewing room to watch the movie—I believe it was *City Slickers*—he handed me his number and asked if I would have lunch with him. I wasn't quite sure what to make of his invitation, as our age difference was quite formidable.

A few weeks passed. I called Tony, but before agreeing to lunch plans, I said, "I think you are a little too old for me. Why are you asking me to lunch?"

"I don't want to date you. I want to paint you," he replied.

I was relieved—until I found out he wanted to paint me in the nude. Though I was flattered, I politely declined the offer. Years later, I laughed when I heard that his paintings were going for a lot of money—to think, I could have been in one of them!

Many nights, I would walk into parties in Hollywood mansions, amazed by how much cocaine was lined up on the coffee tables. I would make my way through the crowd of coked-out people, stumbling as they went for their next line.

I never really fit into the Hollywood crowd—I had never tried a cigarette, much less drugs, with the exception of maybe a marijuana contact high from riding with my neighbor to high school. People accepted me and told me they respected my decision to keep it clean, but they would usually tell me this when they were completely stoned out of their minds. I didn't care that the path I was choosing was different. I liked to pave my own path, and I would enjoy the journey that I knew lay before me.

One day I was telling Randy, another music business friend I'd met through Charlie, about all the crazy things I had seen and experienced since moving to Los Angeles, and he said to me, "You are going to have the ride of your life. Pretty girls get to do whatever they want in LA."

All I knew was that I felt fortunate to be living the life that I was and to be experiencing all the things I was being exposed to. There was never a dull moment. Certainly, when you were dating in Los Angeles, you never knew quite what to expect. There was the time I was meeting a friend for lunch in Westwood at her office. As I walked into the elevator, I met this attractive Italian man. We spoke for only a few minutes before he got out of the elevator and I continued to the top floor to meet my friend. When we returned to her office after lunch, the receptionist handed me a business card and said a guy had been looking for me. It turned out the man I'd met in the elevator had gone to every floor in the building, all twenty-one of them, to find out who I was.

Another time, I was driving down Santa Monica Boulevard in West Hollywood with the top down in my car—by now, I'd bought a Jaguar convertible. A guy pulled up next to me in a brand new Mercedes at a red light. I could see him out of the corner of my eye trying to get my attention, but I wanted nothing to do with him. At the next red light, he pulled his car in front of mine and stopped, got out of his car, walked to my window, smiled, and said, "I am not going to move my car until you agree to have dinner with me." Glad there was no one behind me, I backed my car up and went around him.

Back east, men were much more reserved, not as aggressive. Yet I had to give the guys in LA credit for trying. After all, it was a big city, and their approaches were certainly interesting. I dated some guys and had some relationships, but none felt quite right. I liked men who were confident but not too confident, humble, and knew how to treat a woman. That man hadn't come along yet, but I could wait. I was having the time of my life.

CHAPTER FIVE

I had been living in LA for about a year and having a lot of fun, but it was time to start thinking about what I was going to do with my life. Charlie said I had a talent for picking out artists worthy of signing, and he tried recruiting me to A&R, or "artist and repertoire." I was flattered that he thought I was capable of finding and developing new talent for a record label, when such a job involved flying to small towns and staying in motels and going to bars to listen to prospective artists. I couldn't see myself doing that. I was happy hanging with the A&R guys and going to see the artists play in Los Angeles. The job has changed a lot since then, thanks to the internet.

I had given up my childhood dream of being a doctor, because I knew that, with a brain tumor, it wasn't possible. Around this time, my medication seemed to be failing, as I was having more frequent seizures. How could I consider going to med school when I could have a seizure and forget what I had just read?

It occurred to me that all I seemed to spend my time doing was organizing and planning my day. That's when I happened to meet a friend for lunch in Beverly Hills, and he asked me to help organize the launch of his hair-care line in Mexico City. It was perfect timing, because I had no idea what I was going to do with my life. Maybe this job might give me direction.

The following month, I traveled to Mexico to launch the hair-care line in a very posh area of the capital. I stayed at what was supposed to be the nicest hotel in town. As I lay in my room, I took in my surroundings—the prints on the walls, the bedding, the furniture. It was all anonymous looking and dull. I could have been in any hotel anywhere in the world. How boring! An idea came to me: what if a hotel could be more than just a place to rest your head at night? What if it was an *experience?* At that moment, I came up with an idea for my own business: I would transform five-star hotels into unforgettable experiences for their guests. My first client was the Beverly Hills Hotel, and from those beginnings I went on to work on many of the boutique hotels all across America.

My office was in a great location, close to Rodeo Drive. I had a blast and met a lot of interesting people, such as the man who is widely credited with turning Rodeo Drive into a luxury shopping mecca, Fred Hayman. He had founded, and now owned, the fashion boutique Giorgio Beverly Hills. Fred was always charming, and he traveled to work with his

German shepherd—there his dog would be, right next to his desk, during our meetings. We sat going over the importance of the signature yellow that made the Giorgio brand instantly recognizable. I was meeting with him to have high-end robes and towels manufactured for him, and Fred stressed to me that the yellow had to be matched exactly, or he wouldn't accept the order. Luckily, the factory returned the samples exactly to his standards, and all went well. Working with Fred Hayman was like entering a time warp and being transported to old Hollywood, an era that always appealed to me.

I was in my office in Beverly Hills in 1992 when I heard the jury had acquitted four Los Angeles police officers that had been on trial for the beating of Rodney King after a high-speed pursuit. The riots that erupted were the biggest that had been seen in the United States since those in the 1960s in Detroit and the Watts neighborhood of LA. No matter what news station I tuned to, there was constant coverage of the looting, arson, and civil disturbances that had begun in South Central Los Angeles and swept across the city, as thousands of people joined the rioting over the next six days.

When I heard reports that looters were making their way to Beverly Hills, I walked next door to the police department. The officers' response to my concerns was "Let them try." There were police on every corner of every street surrounding Beverly Hills, guns in hand, but later that day it seemed the rioting and looting were escalating throughout the city, so I decided it would be better to go home. That night I sat on my eleventh-floor balcony in the Wilshire Corridor between Beverly Hills and Westwood, looking out over Century City, watching fires burning as far as the eye could see.

It was only when the situation seemed to be completely out of control, and the local police could no longer handle it, that the California Army National Guard and the 1st Marine Division were called in. Fifty-three people were killed during the riots, more than 2,000 people were injured, and the property damage was estimated at over $1 billion.

Growing up in Maryland and Virginia, I never imagined that I would experience anything like the rioting that paralyzed Los Angeles. The continual threat of earthquakes was also new for me, and I experienced my first serious tremor in 1994. At around 4:30 a.m., I was awoken by the most intense shaking I had ever felt. I was still living in a high-rise on Wilshire Boulevard, between Beverly Hills and Westwood, and the walls of my apartment were almost all glass. As I made my way down the hallway to get to the support beam between the dining room and kitchen, I was thrown from one wall to the other. As I made it to the end of the hallway, I looked out the window and saw transformers exploding across the city. I watched everything from downtown Los Angeles all the way to the beach go completely dark in one clean sweep. Then the car alarms started going off.

The earthquake, with a magnitude of 6.7, went on for less than a minute, but it felt like forever. I lived on one of the upper floors of the building and had no idea if there was structural damage. It was some time before the residents were given the okay to leave the building. As soon as I could, I drove to Beverly Hills see if there was any damage at my office. On the streets, it was complete chaos.

In my office, everything had been thrown from the shelves. Looking around, I could see that the building had sustained quite a bit of damage. It didn't seem safe, so I walked out my office door to leave. I was confronted by the sight of a guard dog at the end of the hallway. The woman who had the office next to mine was well known for manufacturing crystal handbags, and she would leave her dog to protect the valuables in her office. In the chaos of the quake, the dog had escaped, and now he was blocking the exit. As I approached, he began to show teeth. I slowly backed into my office and tried to dial the dog's owner. The phone lines were dead. There I stood at the door, peeking out. I hoped the dog would walk down the hall so I could slip out, and I prayed that the building wouldn't come down on top of me. I waited there about an hour until he left, and then I made a mad dash to the door, dreading that he might return and attack me.

The weeks that followed were incredibly stressful. I had meetings planned all over the city, and a portion of the 10 Freeway had collapsed, which was my usual route to downtown Los Angeles. The thing I remember the most from those days was the fear of having to drive through the most dangerous, crime-ridden areas of LA to get to my meetings, always making sure I left enough room in front of my car in case I needed to get away fast.

Around this time, my seizures grew out of control, and I began to have a hard time concentrating at work, so I arranged an appointment with one of the top neurologists at the UCLA hospital. After asking me a litany of questions, he gave me a list of tests to have done. As I was leaving the room, he said, "Don't worry—I will make you better." I believe that was the moment UCLA became part of my family.

I went through a battery of tests, from EEGs to MRIs, and was put on different medications for my seizures, with no success. Though the doctors I'd seen as a teenager had said the tumor was inoperable, at UCLA they raised the possibility of having brain surgery to remove it. First, I would need to have some more tests to see if I was a suitable candidate.

I had never been afraid of medical procedures before, always looking at each test and treatment as if it were just a bump in the road—but brain surgery was different. There was so much more at stake. What if something went wrong during the operation?

First I had the Wada test, which is used to determine which side of a patient's brain is responsible for speech and memory. They inserted a catheter into my groin, leading all the way up to my carotid arteries, which supply blood to the brain. When a barbiturate was injected into the right artery, the right side of my brain went to sleep, but I was still able to speak and follow directions. About fifteen minutes later, when the drug had worn off, they injected it into the left carotid artery to put that side of my brain to sleep. Within seconds, I was unable to speak and I couldn't see—everything went black. It was like something out of a science fiction movie, and I was fully awake to experience it all.

My tumor was on the right side of my brain, and because the test results showed that my memory and speech were on the left side, that meant they would be able to operate. But I wasn't approved for surgery just yet. The next round of testing required me to stop taking my seizure medication and be admitted to the hospital. There, they placed electrodes on my scalp, which collected data about my brain activity. The data were transmitted to a room across the hall, and a video camera was directed on me at all times so they could see when I was having a seizure. For almost a month, I remained in bed, with the heavy electrodes strapped to the top of my head, their lines leading to a metal box. Finally, they had gathered enough information to know which parts of my brain were experiencing the greatest seizure activity. It was a miserable experience. Not only am I a person who doesn't like to sit, but at times I was having more than seventy-five seizures a day. I was in a business partnership and also living with my boyfriend at the time, David. Though I would have much preferred to be at the office, he was running the business while I was stuck in the hospital.

While the doctors analyzed the data they had collected, I was finally allowed to leave my bed and roam the halls with my IV. Having always had a passion for medicine, I was usually fascinated by what I observed in hospitals over the years. However, one day when I was roaming the halls with my IV and happened to look into a room, I witnessed something I had never seen before, too gruesome to explain. I asked the nurse what had happened to the man in the bed, and she told me he had suffered a grand mal seizure while driving a motorcycle and had ridden off the edge of an overpass, landing onto a moving vehicle below. It made me even more determined to do whatever it took to have a life free of seizures.

Finally, I was allowed to go home, and my brain surgery was scheduled. The day couldn't come soon enough for me, especially after I had a grand mal seizure in the bath. I can vaguely remember coming in and out of consciousness. Things were blurry as I tried to reach for the soap holder, only to fall back and hit my head on the side of the bathtub. When the seizure ended, I was left with a large bump and bruise on my head and blood in the water, but I knew it could have been so much worse. I had thought many times throughout my life just how lucky I had been, some days joking that there must be an army of angels following me around to protect me. I knew the statistics: because I might have a seizure, I was fifteen to nineteen times more likely than others to drown while bathing. I wasn't going to allow fear to stop me, though, because I believe that fear is what we make it.

My father flew in to be at my side when the big day finally arrived. As I was wheeled into surgery at six o'clock in the morning, I don't remember having a moment of fear. All I felt was excitement about the life I could possibly have after the surgery. The pre-op room was cold and sterile. The anesthesiologist was by my side, asking me a lot of questions, and nurses were coming in and out, connecting machines and lines to me. "When are they going to shave my head?" I kept wondering. The last thing I remember was a nurse inserting an IV, and before I knew it, I was waking up in the ICU. Everything was blurry, and I was trying to make sense of it all. It seemed like it took forever for me to be able to think clearly. It was now night; I had just lost an entire day of my life.

The following day, my father told me that when he came to visit me in the ICU after the surgery and asked how I was doing, I said, "Bad hurt bad," as if I had reverted back to being a child. I don't remember saying that; really, I don't remember much about that night except for being in an incredible amount of pain.

As the week progressed, the pain started to ease a bit, but the nurses waking me every hour on the hour to take my vitals started to get old. I am a light sleeper, and it was difficult getting back to sleep after they left the room, so on the seventh day I asked the surgeon if I could be released from the hospital early. Because I lived down the street from the hospital, on the eighth day he let me go home. I wasn't sure I was ready . . . but I could never have imagined just how hard it was going to be. Still in a lot of pain, I wasn't able to stand for longer than five minutes before having to lie down and rest. It took me more than a half hour to make a peanut butter and jelly sandwich. Because I had gone through so much medically already, I thought that I could do this on my own, so I had told David he should go to work. I must have been crazy to not have someone at the house to help me. Just before my surgery, David had given me a Maltese dog, which I'd called Nicky. He was a tiny little ball of fur weighing maybe one pound when I picked him up at the breeder's home in Beverly Hills, and I fell in love with him from the first minute. He was so affectionate; he always stuck with me and followed at my feet wherever I went. When I got back from the hospital, I would lie in bed, and Nicky would curl up next to my head, as if he knew that I was in pain and was trying to protect me.

I managed to doze off for a couple of hours the first night, but when I woke the following morning, my vision was blurry, and there was gurgling in my lungs. The surgeon told me to meet him in the emergency room right away. There, they put me through tests for the next eleven hours. Still unable to figure out what was causing my symptoms, at the twelfth hour they did a spinal tap. Only they did it incorrectly and had to redo the procedure. The results of the second test came back negative, and the doctor decided it was best to release me. I was exhausted and in a lot of pain, but I was aware enough to know they were missing something.

The next morning, I woke at home groggy, unable to move, and in terrible pain if I attempted to move. A few hours later, my temperature had reached 103 degrees, and I had a headache that was so severe I had never felt that kind of pain in my entire life. I lay there crying, putting a pillow over my head, and asking for David's help. He kept calling the surgeon, who said that my symptoms were most likely from having had two spinal taps. He called in prescriptions for David to pick up.

None of the medications worked, and I got worse overnight. That morning, just as David was preparing to call the surgeon, the hospital called to say they had run the test again on the sample they had taken during the second spinal tap. I had bacterial meningitis.

I was rushed to UCLA and put on antibiotics and medication to reduce my fever. I lay there wondering how this could be happening to me again. Could I survive this infection twice?

At the hospital, they discovered that during the first spinal tap, they had gone too deep and brought blood into my spinal column. I spent the next two weeks in the hospital, and to the surprise of the doctors, I recovered completely. Once again, I knew I had been very lucky. Yet every time I came through a medical crisis, I would feel a sense of guilt for some time, wondering why I was spared and questioning my purpose. I arrived home, and all I wanted to do was sit in a hot bath. As I undressed and saw myself in the mirror, I stood there in shock at what I saw. I was covered in bruises from where they had drawn blood. When I was readmitted for the meningitis, there weren't many veins left that hadn't been used from the brain surgery, so they had to draw blood from my legs and sometimes my feet and toes.

A week passed and I woke to a sunny morning. As I made my way to the kitchen, I realized I was starting to feel better. I sat on the balcony overlooking the city and felt an overwhelming sense of boredom from being cooped up in the hospital and my apartment for so long. I called my friend Michael to come get me.

When Michael arrived and I opened the door, he could hardly say a word as he stared at me: I was bald, with monster metal stitches that wrapped around the entire right side of my head, and my face was still swollen as a side effect of medication. We drove to a local coffee shop, and along the way Michael asked me twice, "Are you sure you don't want to wear a wig or a hat?"

I laughed and said, "If someone has a problem with how I look, then it's their problem. I'm just glad to be alive."

At the coffee shop, people did stare, and a few kids even came up to ask what happened to me. I told them a wild story to make it more interesting. It was the most liberated I had ever felt in my entire life. In a town that is utterly preoccupied with how people look, I had chosen not to worry about what others thought of my appearance. I let the world see me as I truly was—and the world didn't come to an end. This experience changed how I would think about beauty for the rest of my life.

A few weeks passed, and I went back to work, though I knew I would need to take it easy for a while. The first two weeks were rough, but I was determined to get my life back to normal. A new normal. My life was changing; I felt like a different person. I was melancholy at times. I had also come to the sad realization that my relationship with David was never going to lead to marriage. We would remain business partners, but on a personal level, it was time that we went our separate ways. I packed my belongings and moved into a new apartment in Beverly Hills, ready to start a new stage of my life.

CHAPTER SIX

One night after returning home from work to my Beverly Hills apartment, I lay in the bath in tears. I had been given a new life free of seizures; and at twenty-six, I had my whole life ahead of me. But there was something missing. There was something I still needed to complete me. I wanted to fall madly in love. I lay there, praying I would meet the man I would fall in love with and give my heart to. I'd had some great romances and relationships, but something always seemed to be wrong. The guys I was attracted to were often older than me, in their thirties or forties, and they were focused more on their careers than on relationships. Or when the honeymoon period was over, it turned out there just wasn't enough in the relationship to move forward.

Two months later, my friend Carrie asked me to go on a blind date. She would be there with her boyfriend, Rick, and one of his friends, a professional photographer named Bruce.

"A blind date in Los Angeles? No way," I said. It was hard enough to date guys in LA when you'd already met them in person.

"Rick says he's really cute," Carrie said.

"You're probably just saying that to get me to go on the date," I replied, laughing.

After a few minutes of her coaxing me, I caved. Who knew, maybe it could be interesting, I thought.

We went for dinner at a popular restaurant in Beverly Hills. Carrie led me through the crowd to the bar, where Rick and Bruce were sitting. As we got to the bar, Bruce quickly stood up, introduced himself, and gave me a hug. I can picture that moment like it was yesterday. He had this crazy curly light brown hair shot through with salt and pepper, and a big smile. I could tell he was really nervous, because he didn't seem to know what to do next, so I asked if I could sit down. Realizing he'd missed that one, he fumbled with the bar stool a bit and had me sit down next to him. Our conversation took off instantly and was comfortable right from the moment I sat down, as if we had been longtime friends. Rick had been right: Bruce was cute.

I was surprised I felt attracted to him. I had never really been interested in artists before; I had always dated men who were corporate. What had I been missing? It didn't take long before I could see Bruce had a big heart, and halfway through the dinner, I knew there was something special about this man. Of course, it didn't hurt that he had the most beautiful blue eyes that you could get lost in.

As our conversation continued, we became lost in our own world, almost forgetting at times that our friends were there, too. I couldn't help it. I found myself wanting to know more about this man, who was different from anyone I had dated before. We didn't say it, but we both knew there was something between us. There was nothing more attractive to me than a man who was handsome and didn't know it. When a man was smart and humble on top of that, he was truly a rare find.

After dinner, Bruce and Rick walked me and Carrie to my car. Bruce asked if he could give me a kiss, and just as I was saying "Yes," he held me and gave me the most amazing kiss. He asked me on another date the following night, and after that kiss, of course I said, "Yes."

As Carrie and I got in my car, he stopped me and said, "I'm not ready for this date to end. Would you meet us for drinks?" We followed Bruce and Rick to the Hotel Bel Air, and before we knew it, we were closing the bar.

For our date the next evening, Bruce took me back to the Hotel Bel Air, and we dined alongside the pond, where swans glided across the water. He was the perfect gentleman, careful to make sure that every move he made was the right one.

"Would you like to try what I'm having?" he asked when our meals came, and as I nodded, he reached across the table and fed me from his fork. Then I passed my fork to his lips. There was a gentleness in his care that made me feel as though we had been together for years.

After dinner, he drove me into Hollywood. I had no idea where he was taking me, and I didn't care—I was excited to see what was next. We arrived at the Magic Castle Hotel and had drinks overlooking the city. We held hands and kissed.

"Thank you for arranging such a special evening for me," I said when we were leaving, walking back toward the valet.

"Ah, but the evening isn't over yet," Bruce said, smiling.

He drove me to a legendary old dive bar on Hollywood Boulevard, the Frolic Room. As he opened the door for me, he said, "I used to come to this place all the time back when I was a starving young photographer."

As we walked in, I knew Bruce was trying to test me to see how down to earth I really was. It was a great test, too. The Frolic Room was a dark, old, dirty bar, but I was game. There I sat at the bar, in a nice dress, and I'm sure I stood out. I was getting a glimpse of how versatile he was: he could be at home in a five-star restaurant one minute, a dive bar the next. I found that facet of his personality very attractive.

Earlier in the night, I had asked if he would one day show me some of his photographs, and as we left the bar, he said, "So, would you like to come and see some of my work?"

I said "Yes," so he drove me to his house by the beach. It was a sweet old house, and when we walked in, it felt as if it was giving me a hug.

"When I started making money in photography, I was looking for a house to rent, and I came to see this one. It was so ugly, I almost drove off, but I saw the potential," he told me.

"A couple of years passed, the owner sadly fell on hard times, and I bought it from him."

As I looked around, I could see that it was a bit of a bachelor pad. It needed a woman's touch and some love.

We sat on the sofa in the living room, and he handed me photographs to look at. Each was so different from the one before—a slick stock image of a boardroom, which he explained was his biggest seller; glossy Playboy ads; portrait shots of Hollywood producers; sportspeople such as Bruce Jenner and Martina Navratilova; jazz musicians such as Dizzy Gillespie; and actors including Ted Danson, Kate Jackson, and Martin Landau.

I sat back on the sofa, looked at him, and said, "You are really good."

"I know," he said, with a cocky tone.

"And humble, too!" I said, and laughed. He had a great sense of humor, and my favorite kind: dry sarcasm.

"If I hadn't already seen that you are a good guy, I probably would never go out with you again," I teased.

"Then I'm so glad you saw that," he replied softly.

We told each other about our lives, and I began to feel a connection with him that I had never felt with anyone before. Bruce had been born in the Philippines and lived there until he was thirteen; then he moved with his family to Tokyo. At nineteen, he moved from Japan to Los Angeles to go to college to study business. A friend of his decided to go to Sydney and asked if Bruce wanted to join him. Realizing he wasn't interested in getting a business degree, Bruce quit school and jumped on a plane to Australia. When Bruce's father, an executive for a large shipping company, found out, he cut him off. Needing money, Bruce got a job working as an assistant to a photographer. His first day at work, he picked up the camera and knew at that moment what he was supposed to do for the rest of his life. He traveled back to Los Angeles, bought a camera, and started taking photos.

Bruce's friend Gerard let him live in a room in his photography studio. Eventually, he landed jobs photographing famous actors and musicians. When an Englishman, Tony Stone, came to America to start what would become a highly successful stock photography company, he approached Bruce to shoot high-end commercial photos. Bruce was just getting by at the time, and he jumped at the chance to earn some extra money, not knowing just how lucrative the stock-image business would be for him. His style would become known as "lifestyle photography," and he would shoot anything from a board meeting to something as crazy as a hefty man wearing a bathing suit, sitting in an inner tube in a swimming pool with a drink in his hand.

As he felt he had achieved what he wanted in stock photography, he decided to move into shooting stock video clips that could be sold for commercial use. It seemed that he always had the Midas touch and that everything he set out to pursue brought him success. He had believed in himself enough to do what it took to become successful, and he'd done it on his own terms, without the help of his parents.

He told me wild stories from when he was a teen in Tokyo—late nights out with friends in the city, his parents oblivious to what he was getting himself into. It was the 1960s, and drugs were a part of the culture. He confessed that he certainly tried most of them but found that drugs weren't for him and walked away from the scene. It was hard for me to imagine that such a Zen, easygoing guy could have been so wild.

"It was an escape from my life," he said. Only much later, when he had shared with me stories about his early life, when his mother and father had fought a lot, would I come to understand why he wanted to escape.

I couldn't help but feel envious that he was born in the 1950s. For some reason, everything about that period seemed very familiar and comfortable to me. Later, when we had gotten to know each other better, Bruce told me stories about his childhood, and suddenly I pictured a scene in my mind, in black and white. It was Bruce and his mother, walking down a sidewalk in the Philippines, and as we passed each other, we made eye contact. Who knows, maybe our souls had traveled lifetimes together. Maybe that is why we felt so comfortable together from the moment we met.

It was getting late. As we realized that it was time for him to take me home, he looked at me and said with great conviction, "I know that I have known you my entire life." At that moment, I knew I was going to fall madly in love with this man, and he was the only one I would ever want to be with.

As he pulled up in front of my house, I thanked him for giving me the most special date of my life. We parked, and he walked me to my door. He pulled me close to him and, while pressing his body against mine, gave me a long, passionate kiss.

"I wish this evening never had to end," he said. I didn't say it, but I didn't want the evening to end, either.

I walked inside and closed the door. A few moments later, I opened the door—to find that he was still standing there, with a smile. I invited him in, and he stayed with me that night as if we had known each other for years. I didn't sleep the entire night; I just lay there next to him, holding his hand as he slept and thanking God for answering my prayer.

What I would be willing to give for the chance to go back to that day and relive it all over again.

☆   ☆   ☆

The next morning, he left for a meeting. Two hours later, he called and said, "I miss you. Will you have lunch with me?"

At first I thought, this guy is crazy! But I liked that he liked me that much and wanted to spend all of his time with me. I had all but given up on meeting a guy who knew how to love me with everything he had.

During lunch, we talked about how strangely parallel our lives were. There was the Japanese connection in our backgrounds, which meant we understood the culture that each of us had grown up with. We both spoke Japanese, though Bruce was much more fluent than I was. And we both had the same beliefs and morals. It felt as though we were always destined to meet, that none of it was by chance.

In the middle of the conversation, when I least expected it, Bruce said, "I know this might sound crazy, but will you move in with me? Last night was great, and I felt comfortable with you. I want to wake with you every day."

Instantly, I knew that I felt the same about him. "Yes!" I said.

It wasn't like me to rush in so quickly. The beginning of a relationship was always the most exciting part for me, when a guy would romance and charm me. I've had a man surprise me with a flight on a private plane just so we could have dinner and sit on the beach for the evening. With another guy I dated in D.C., I went away for a weekend in New Orleans, but the morning we were supposed to catch our return flight, we couldn't bear to return to the cold, so we jumped on a flight to Cancun. We had nothing to wear, so we each bought a bathing suit, shorts, and a t-shirt and then spent the week lying on the beach. I wasn't the type to fast-forward through all that and cut straight to a serious relationship. But with Bruce, it was different. He was connected to my soul, and I knew he wouldn't be like the ones who'd come before him.

So there he was the next day at my house, picking up my boxes so I could move in with him. The entire day, I kept thinking, this is nuts, I have only known him four days. Yet at the same time, it felt so right.

The next morning, we woke and lay in bed most of the day. When we finally got up to eat, I discovered just how right I was about Bruce's home needing a woman's touch: even a church mouse would have starved in his kitchen. We ordered in Thai food and sat eating it in the living room, he in his boxers and I in a pair of his boxers and a t-shirt.

Knowing that I love music, he walked over to the stereo and put on one of his favorite songs, "The Stars Are Ours," by The Nylons. He came back, grabbed my hand and pulled me to my feet. He drew my body close to his, and we began to dance. He played DJ for the next few hours, and we lay on the sofa holding one another, laughing and talking. I couldn't have imagined wanting to be anywhere else.

CHAPTER SEVEN

How easy it was for us to fall into each other's lives at a time when we both needed each other. I was still regaining my health after going through brain surgery and meningitis, while Bruce was exhausted from working like a maniac for the past ten years, rushing from one photo shoot to the next. I could tell he needed someone who would love and care for him. But when we first met, he was fiercely independent, and I knew it would take some time before he got used to sharing his life.

We would have to get used to each other's quirks, too. Bruce was a laid-back kind of guy, and I was more high energy, always on the go. Gradually, we found a middle ground. I learned to relax a bit more, and my high energy helped him get motivated. Though he was once a night owl, he now started waking at 8:00 AM.

One beautiful sunny Saturday afternoon soon after I moved in, we went to Beverly Hills for lunch and afterward found ourselves in Neiman Marcus. He needed a makeover; he was ready for a change and for someone to show him he was special. We spent the day running around Beverly Hills, joking that he was the "Pretty Man" in this film. Once he had his new wardrobe, I could tell he felt better about himself. He had a smile in his eyes, knowing that someone wanted to care.

When I would get dressed, I'd show him what I was wearing and, like most women, would say, "Does my butt look fat in this?" He would always say, "Yes," just to make me laugh. Sometimes, he would do this little dance and sing, "You have a big butt, and I cannot lie." When I would ask him something, he would laugh and say, "Yes, dear, whatever you want." I'd always reply with, "Smart man."

One of the greatest joys Bruce found in his life was playing tennis. It was the only thing that I knew could get him out of bed early in the morning. I would joke with him and say, "If you had to choose between me and tennis, I'm pretty sure you would choose tennis." He would always laugh and say, "I'm glad that I can have both."

We played a lot of tennis together. He loved teaching, and I learned a lot from him, but every time we played, he would always ask me, "Why do you have to put the death grip on your racket?" No matter what he did to show me how to hold the racket, I could never manage to get it right.

I would say his first love was hopefully me; second, tennis; and third, watching movies, especially ones that had dark themes. He liked to try to figure out the mind that was behind the film and what the filmmaker must have been thinking. I didn't like those films—but thankfully he didn't mind watching them alone, because he loved his quiet time. Still, I could get him to watch my chick flicks. I know he hated them, but he did it for me.

We hadn't been living together very long when Bruce was sent to London for a shoot. When he returned, he announced, "I am ready to retire and spend my time with you. Would you like that?"

"Yes!" I said. "But won't you get bored?" After all, he was only forty-four and in the midst of a successful career.

"If we need a break, I'll just go play tennis," he said. "But I'm not completely done yet. One day, when I'm older, I want to produce a feature film."

I would miss watching him work. It was a real turn-on to see him at big photo shoots. As he took photos, there was something sexy about him—yes, he was very talented, but his humbleness was what really turned me on. Bruce possessed a talent that was given to him at birth, and he was lucky enough to have discovered his passion. But what I found most impressive was his ease as he assembled large photo shoots and just how kind he was to everyone he worked with, which in Los Angeles can be quite rare.

For me, work was busier than ever, and I often got home late. On days when I was tired and didn't want to figure out what to make for dinner, I would choose a restaurant and be about to call and order before I realized I couldn't face the nightmare of trying to find parking. He would always say, "Just call it in, I'll go pick it up." He didn't care about the parking—he would just deal with it and never complain. He always seemed to know what to do to make my life a bit easier.

One day, I arrived home from work and found Bruce sitting in the living room. I joined him and asked if he wanted to take me for a drive, because it was a perfect warm evening to put the top down and drive up the coast. We found ourselves in Malibu and decided to stop and have a drink. I had to be at work early the next morning, so we headed back when it started to get late. Bruce pulled in and parked at the end of our driveway and came around to open my door. As I stepped out to walk toward the house, he stopped and held me and told me he loved me for the first time.

I don't think there is a day that goes by that I don't look at that spot on the driveway and think about that night. There are special moments I will never forget in life, and that will always be one of them.

☆   ☆   ☆

For our first Thanksgiving dinner, Bruce decided he was going to make the dinner. I was usually the one who cooked, but I was excited for him to take charge. But on Thanksgiving morning, as I helped him get all the groceries out of the refrigerator, I realized he had purchased a frozen turkey and hadn't taken it out the day before so it could thaw. It was like my parents' first Thanksgiving all over again! I got on the phone and, to my complete surprise, was able to find a store that was open where

I could buy a fresh turkey. I rushed off to pick it up, while he got on with preparing everything else. When I arrived back at the house with the turkey, I was greeted with a big thank-you kiss, and it was all worth it for that moment. Needless to say, we were way behind schedule, and we ended up having dinner at midnight. No one seemed to care, though, and we had a great story to tell for years to come.

The next day, Bruce said to me, "Sweetie, I wanted to do something special for your birthday, the first birthday I've celebrated with you. And our first Christmas Day together."

What had he planned that was so special he needed to tell me almost a month in advance?

I gasped when he handed me an itinerary. He was taking me to Austria.

In Salzburg, he had arranged for us to stay in a beautiful old hunting lodge that was nestled in the mountains, by a lake. After we settled into our room, I walked over, gave him a hug, and with eyes full of tears thanked him for doing something so special.

"This is the nicest thing anyone has ever done for me," I told him.

We lay in bed until it was time to get dressed and walk to the restaurant for Christmas Eve dinner, which is the traditional way to celebrate Christmas in Austria. The restaurant was beautifully decorated for the holidays, and I felt like I had stepped into a fairy tale. At the end of the celebrations, we went back to our room, but we were so jet-lagged that neither of us could sleep.

Around midnight, Bruce got out of bed and got dressed. "Come on," he said. "Bundle up, we're going for a walk."

"Are you crazy?" I said, cozy in the warm bed. "It's freezing outside!" It was barely above zero degrees.

"But it's so beautiful outside," he said, parting the curtains to show me the view out the window.

He kept up his persuasion until I gave in. I put on all my layers, and out the door we went.

Walking down to the lake under a big moon, with snow falling, I knew he was right. The evening couldn't have been more beautiful or romantic. Having lived in Los Angeles for years, I wasn't properly prepared for this kind of cold, but I didn't care any longer. Actually, it was a great excuse to snuggle closer to Bruce. We stopped and stared at a snow-covered mountain, and as I looked over at him, the moon lit up his face. I realized just how much I was falling in love with him. Being with him, I no longer felt alone. My life had never felt more complete. Up until that moment, I never knew that such a love could have existed.

We strolled until we were no longer able to feel our fingers and toes. Back in our room, Bruce reached into his bag and pulled out a small gift box and an envelope.

"Go on, open it," he said, as he handed me the gift. I opened the box, and inside were three gold rings. From the envelope, he pulled out a letter and began to read it to me.

"My dearest Melissa, there are no words that can express the love I feel for you and how grateful I am to have found you.

"On the occasion of your 26th year:

When you wear the first ring, remember a white Christmas in Austria;

When you wear the second ring, remember I truly love you;

When you wear the third ring, remember I will always be your friend."

I stood blinking away tears, touched by the beauty of his gift and the love in the words he had expressed to me.

"Thank you from the bottom of my heart," I whispered, slipping the stackable rings on my finger. I knew that every time I wore them, I would think of this moment.

I hadn't expected such a thoughtful gift. After all, we had just met! I handed him the gift I had bought for him and said, "I'm sorry, my gift pales in comparison to the gift you have given me, but please know this comes from my heart."

He opened the box, and inside was a watch he had admired one day in a store.

"Turn it over," I said. On the back, I'd had inscribed, "I will love you for eternity." No truer words could have ever been written.

We spent days walking through Salzburg, toured Mozart's home, and ate until we couldn't fit into our clothes any longer. Next thing I knew, he was telling me to pack, because we were going on the train somewhere else. He wouldn't tell me where. Then we boarded the train, traveling through the night in a romantic sleeper car, lying next to each other. We arrived in Vienna and checked into a grand hotel in the middle of the city.

When we woke the next morning and walked into the restaurant for breakfast, we were overcome by cigarette smoke so thick you could practically cut through it. It was astonishing how many people were smoking so early in the morning, and while eating. We soon found it was the same everywhere in Vienna.

That night was New Year's Eve, and all I knew before we left Los Angeles was to bring a formal gown for the occasion. I didn't know what Bruce had planned, and I didn't mind, because I love surprises. We got dressed up: I was in a long black gown, and I wore black silk gloves and my mother's Mikimoto pearls and earrings. Bruce was very handsome in an Armani tuxedo. He took me to a special dinner at the Vienna opera house, which was a truly magnificent place.

At the stroke of midnight, he looked at me and said, "Happy New Year, beautiful. I look forward to spending the rest of my life with you."

Lost in the moment, we kissed, and I said, "Me, too."

It truly was the most magical trip I had ever been on, and it was made even more special by the fact that Bruce had known me for only a few months, and I already meant so much to him that he wanted to create an experience I would never forget.

Even though I had a great time on our trip to Austria, there had been moments when a deep sadness came over me. I might wake in the morning feeling happy, and then suddenly I would feel like someone had just died. I couldn't explain why, because I couldn't understand these feelings. I kept them to myself until we were on the plane heading back to Los Angeles, when I confided in Bruce that I had been having dark, sorrowful feelings for no reason throughout the trip.

Maybe I was having a different form of seizure than I'd had before. As soon as I got home, I set up an appointment with my neurologist.

"You're not having seizures—you're grieving," the doctor said after he'd examined me.

"Sorry, I don't quite understand," I replied.

"You have spent your entire life taking care of the other person inside of you with seizures. Now that part of you is gone, and you no longer have seizures; you are relearning how to live your life without them. It takes time, but you will be okay," he assured me.

I left the hospital relieved to have an answer. At the same time, there was a lingering feeling of sadness. There was a part of me that wanted my old life back with seizures, maybe because it was familiar to me.

It took a while for me to believe that the seizures were actually gone. A few months passed, and I realized that I was no longer living with the ever-present concern that I would have a seizure in public and have to cover it up. And it turned out that my doctor was correct: I began to no longer feel the loss of the old me.

CHAPTER EIGHT

Of course, the honeymoon stage couldn't last forever. At first, perhaps I overlooked telltale signs that beneath the humility that I was so drawn to in this attractive man lay a profound vulnerability.

As our relationship got more serious, I could see that our age difference was weighing on Bruce's mind. I had fallen for him so heavily; I wasn't likely to let our age difference get in the way. Actually, in my eyes, our age difference brought back to his life a youthfulness that he hadn't realized he'd lost. As we walked back from the beach one morning, I led him on a different route home to the one we usually took. When we reached the grassy median of the street, which ran the length of two blocks, he wasn't quite sure what I was up to. I took off my shoes and had him do the same. We walked barefoot through the grass that day like we were kids, and after that, every time we took that route home, he would remove his shoes and walk with me, a smile on his face.

Still, no matter how much I assured Bruce that our age gap didn't bother me, there always seemed to be a lingering insecurity in him.

"One of us could die—none of us knows how much time we have—but when you are sixty, I will be seventy-eight," he said to me one night when we were lying in bed.

"So?" I replied.

"When you are seventy, I will be eighty-eight," he said.

"So?" I again replied.

We lay there for a while in silence in the dark, and I could tell something was on his mind.

"Can I tell you something strange?" he said finally.

"Of course," I said. "Anything."

"I had the same dream over and over again throughout my childhood. I dreamt I was going to die," he said. "And you were there."

I looked into his eyes—and was surprised to see that he was serious. I rolled toward him and said, "Don't worry—you are going to live a long, happy life, and I am going to be right there with you."

"I hope so," he said.

We never spoke about that night again, but from time to time, I would hear his voice in my head, telling me about his dream. I would pray it meant I would be there when we died of old age.

What we didn't know as we lay there that night was that so soon after we had found each other, our bond was to be put to the test by circumstances that were out of our control.

Two weeks later, I went to the UCLA medical center—this time, not for treatment but to give blood. My doctors hadn't okayed me for driving yet, because for a time after my surgery, there was still a risk that my seizures might return. Bruce was driving me home in his brand new Suburban. Suddenly, we were jolted by a violent force. A woman in a Cadillac had run a red light, crashing into my door. My head hit the passenger window—on the same side where I had had brain surgery a year and a half before. The impact was so great, our car was pushed one lane over, into oncoming traffic.

Bruce jumped out of the car to check the other driver, not realizing I had been injured. As soon as he realized I was hurt, he called an ambulance, which rushed me back to UCLA. The doctors were concerned that the impact could have damaged the area of my brain that had been operated on, so I was sent to another hospital, where they had the right equipment to perform a range of brain-function tests.

"A layer of your skull was fractured during the accident," said the doctor when the results came back. "You might need another surgery to repair it."

"Oh, no—I can't imagine having brain surgery again," I groaned.

"Well, I suppose we could wait and see what happens before making a decision," the doctor conceded.

I breathed a sigh of relief that for now, at least, I wasn't going back to the operating room.

But there was more news to come. The hospital had run blood tests, and I was pregnant.

Bruce and I looked at each other, amazed. Soon after we met, we'd talked about how we both wanted to have children. While we hadn't been trying, we weren't trying to prevent it, either.

When the doctor returned later, I knew straight away that something was very wrong.

"We're concerned about the health of the baby," he said. "You were given several drugs and injections during your tests, not to mention what your body went through during the accident."

Everything took on a surreal clarity: the doctor's concerned face; Bruce sitting beside me, his face falling.

"Melissa, I'm sorry, but I have to tell you that the odds are low that your baby would survive. The damage the drugs and tests would have on a fetus are such that we recommend you end the pregnancy."

When the doctor left, Bruce and I sat there devastated, trying to process how this could have happened. When we were finally ready to leave the hospital and go home, the nurse entered the room to schedule the appointment for the procedure, and I just stood there looking at her, completely heartbroken.

That night Bruce and I lay in bed wondering if it was the right decision to end the pregnancy. We decided that, given the doctors' warnings, we really didn't have a choice.

Two days later, we arrived at the hospital for the procedure, and within what seemed like minutes, I was being prepped for surgery. As they wheeled me into the operating room, with tears running down my face, Bruce bent down to give me a hug, and he, too, began to cry.

It turned out that I had made the correct decision in declining surgery to repair my skull. I didn't need any treatment, and I was able to continue living my life even with a layer of my skull fractured. It is a little odd when I lie on that side and hear a crackling sound, but I quickly learned to get used to it.

Yet everything I had been through medically had taken its toll. The brain surgery and meningitis, and now the car accident and losing a baby—it was all just too much for me. And, I would come to realize, too much for Bruce. We had just gone through our first really hard experience together. We were feeling so many emotions, and it began to put pressure on our relationship. We started to bicker. Bruce's patience seemed to have run out with me. It just didn't make sense.

"We need a change of scenery," said Bruce one day. "Let's get away from the city and move somewhere quieter."

One of the reasons I loved LA was that I liked being around people and action, so I wasn't thrilled about the idea of moving somewhere quieter, but if it meant healing our relationship, then I was willing to do it. Within no time, we had purchased a house and were moving to Malibu.

I felt isolated there. Along with the emotional stress that I was feeling after losing the baby, it further strained our relationship. Bruce would say insulting things to me for no apparent reason, and he was quick to lose his temper with me. I would return fire, and the next thing I knew, we would be in the middle of a fight. We would become so exhausted that we retreated to separate rooms to get some quiet. I started questioning whether we could get through this.

Time passed, and things didn't get any better. In the past few years, I had gone through a lot, and I felt I needed some time on my own to get my life back and think about our relationship. I needed a break. Maybe we both did.

As I walked out the door with my bag packed, I could tell Bruce was heartbroken and didn't want me to leave. I didn't want to leave, either, but I was breaking inside from all of the stress. I got into my car, and he ran out to me.

"Stop! Stop, sweetie, please," he said.

Tears rolling down my face, I told him, "I can't do this any longer."

"I don't want you to go," he said. "Please, come back inside so we can talk."

"There is nothing to talk about right now, Bruce. The only way we can get through this is if we have a break, and some peace and quiet," I said. But I could see he was clearly hurting, so I went inside to hear what he had to tell me. We sat on the sofa, and tears began to well up in his eyes.

"Why were you mean to me when you knew I was already hurting?" I asked him.

At first, he couldn't say anything. He just stared at me with tears in his eyes. Finally, he said, "There's something I need to tell you, something that will explain why I've been acting like this toward you." His speech was halting, as though he was having a hard time finding the words to say what he needed to tell me.

"I was deceived by a woman in the past, and it almost destroyed me. I have had trouble trusting women ever since then. I'm sorry for what I've put you through. I love you, Melissa, and I don't want to lose you," he said.

I reached over and gave him a hug. Now it made sense. The speed with which our relationship had taken off, the car accident, my pregnancy, and the loss of the baby—they had stirred up the events of his past. I hurt for him that he had been put through something so awful. "You're having a hard time committing. I get it," I said. "Bruce, I love you enough to wait for you until you're ready to trust again."

I saw that a weight had been lifted from his shoulders. I didn't pressure him for more details; I didn't want him to hurt further.

"I'm so glad you told me," I said. "I'm going to be here for you when you're ready to trust again, but for now, I still believe we need some time apart." Bruce nodded his head sorrowfully.

I moved into an apartment in Beverly Hills, and at first it was exciting to be in a new place. I began making plans with friends, but deep down I missed Bruce, and I couldn't really think about having fun without him. Even though I knew we were only taking a break and that it wasn't the end of our relationship, living apart from him made me feel as if it were over. I tried to get on with my life, but there wasn't a moment when I stopped wondering how he was doing and if he missed me, too.

☆　　☆　　☆

For five years I had been complaining of a lump in my throat when I swallowed, and of feeling wired all the time, as if I had just drunk a pot of coffee. My doctor had drained the lump and had a biopsy performed on the fluid, and the results came back negative. He repeated the biopsy on another occasion, and again it came back with the same results.

"It's nothing to be concerned about," he concluded. "It's probably just a goiter."

In my gut, I knew there was something wrong, so I got a referral to a surgeon. After explaining my symptoms to him, I said, "I think it's cancer."

"How do you know that?" he said.

"I'm not sure; I just know," I told him.

He scheduled me for surgery to have the lump removed. The day of the surgery, I wasn't afraid, but as I lay there waiting for them to take me into the operating room, I wished Bruce was there with me. He didn't know I was having surgery, because I didn't want to call and worry him.

While I was in recovery, the surgeon came and spoke to me. "Well, I think that feeling you had was correct. I saw what appeared to be cancer cells in the surrounding tissue. I've sent the tissue to be biopsied."

A few days passed before my surgeon called to tell me the results. I had thyroid cancer—papillary carcinoma—and he was going to schedule another surgery for the following week.

Even though I didn't show it, inside I was devastated. After all I had gone through, I was facing another medical problem—and an uncertain future. If there was ever a time I needed Bruce, it was now. I called him, and he rushed over to my apartment to be with me.

"Melissa, I don't want you to worry about anything. I promise you, everything will be fine," he said. His being there showed me how much he loved me, and I realized I didn't want to be apart from him another moment. He held me close that night, and all the hell I was experiencing seemed to disappear when I was lying in his arms.

The morning of the second surgery, Bruce was by my side. He recognized my surgeon; he had performed a hernia operation on Bruce years before. The surgeon joked with him, "Would you like to perform the first incision? Don't tell me you haven't wanted to slit her throat before!" We all laughed as they wheeled me in for surgery.

It was Bruce's face that I first saw as I woke in the recovery room. The surgeon came in to tell us he had removed my entire thyroid. I would need to take a radioactive iodine pill to kill any remaining tissue, and my body would emit radiation for two months afterward. I would need to be quarantined for the whole two months.

Even though we had to live apart through my radiation treatment, Bruce was still there for me, calling me throughout the day and night, making sure I was okay. It was the loneliest period of my life, and I was really sick from the treatment. My entire apartment was radioactive, and everyone was prohibited from entering. When I had friends pick up medication for me, they had to place it in my mail slot and leave. I knew it was only for sixty days, but it was as if I had the plague. I just wanted it to be over with and to feel better. What I found strange was that humans were prohibited from being with me, but my Maltese dog, Nicky, who weighed only six pounds, was allowed in the apartment. It didn't make sense, but it was comforting for me to have him there with me when I was sick. My business partner, David, was running the business.

My hormones were a mess, it seemed the medical challenges in my life were never going to end, and I started to lose hope. My emotions were out of control—one minute I was fine, and the next I was frustrated and crying. I had no idea how to handle all of this. Bruce didn't know how to handle what I was going through, either, but he tried the best he could. And there were times when I was hurting and wasn't easy to love. I remember crying on the phone, telling him how much I wished he could be there to hold me. I could hear in his voice how helpless he felt.

He sent me letters, and they helped me get through that dark time. "I know you do not feel good about your health right now, but please remember that on your worst day, you put the most beautiful women in the world to shame. Oh, and by the way, I love your butt," he wrote one day, which got a smile out of me.

As soon as my treatment was over and I'd been declared safe to be with other people, Bruce rushed over to be with me. I had never wanted to be with anyone more in my entire life.

Because I'd had my thyroid removed, I began taking thyroid medication every morning, and I would need to continue doing so for the rest of my life.

At my next post-op appointment, I told the doctor, "Something's wrong. I haven't slept for almost a week."

"It's probably because you had two surgeries in a week, and now your body is getting used to the medication," he reassured me.

Another week passed, and I still hadn't slept. I once again saw the doctor, and this time I explained that I was now experiencing a rapid heartbeat. He still wasn't concerned.

I arrived home late that afternoon, and Bruce was off playing tennis. Strangely, I took a shower when I would normally have taken a bath. As I stood under the warm jet of water, I started to feel light-headed. A feeling of comfort came over me, and the next thing I knew, I was lying on the bottom of the shower, Bruce was standing in front of me, and it was dark outside. He had been calling me for hours on my phone, and when I didn't answer, he got worried and came over to my apartment.

Bruce rushed me to the ER, where they tested my blood. It turned out that I had been prescribed too much thyroid medication and had overdosed. My thyroid hormone levels were dangerously high.

"I've never seen a patient with those levels not go into cardiac arrest," the nurse told me.

They put me on the appropriate dosage, and after a while I began to feel better. But once again, I was left asking myself why it always felt as if I were being tested. What was my purpose? Throughout my life, I had felt someone was watching over me. And once again, I guess heaven wasn't quite ready for me.

CHAPTER NINE

The lease was ending on my apartment. "I don't want you to be alone in that place any longer. Please, let me be the man and allow me to take care of you," Bruce said. "You do so much for me; please let me do that for you." I had always been very independent, and I needed to learn how to be vulnerable again.

Bruce came over to help me pick up my things, and we were once again living together. As we lay in bed, we were glad to be back in each other's arms again, and we spoke of the time we were apart. I told him, "The day I was diagnosed with cancer, I sat alone in my apartment and watched a beautiful sunset, and I thought, 'If I were to die tomorrow, I would have wished you were by my side.'"

Even though I was happy we were together again, living in Malibu was still hard for me. I was a people person, and Malibu was isolated, especially as I had split from my business partner, David, and was running a new company out of our guest house. I had to drive twenty-five miles into town to meet with friends, and it was beginning to wear on me. Bruce didn't mind the isolation and would spend his days playing tennis at Pepperdine University. I tried to make the best of it, but I was becoming more unhappy living so far from town. There was a bad energy in that house from the moment we bought it. It was the house that almost ended our relationship.

Perhaps it had something to do with the isolation I felt in Malibu, but one morning, I woke thinking about my mother and how lonely she must have felt when she married my father and lost contact with everyone in her family except her sister, my aunt Tomiko. I decided to track down Mom's family members in Japan for her. I didn't speak Japanese well enough to handle a conversation, and Bruce's Japanese was rusty, but I picked up the phone and dialed the operators in cities around where she grew up. When the operators found out what I was doing, it was obvious they weren't going to give up until we found her family.

Within a few hours, I had found Mom's brother, my uncle Fumio. What made it even more special was that it was Mother's Day. I knew at that moment, there would never be another gift that I could give Mom to compare to this one. I got as much information as I could about the family from Uncle Fumio. Two brothers had died in the war, a sister had died from cancer, and, sadly, Mom's father had also died.

I had dreamed of taking my mother on a trip to Japan, during which I would surprise her by reuniting her with her family, but because there had been so many deaths, I decided it would be too hard on her. Instead, I gave her the telephone numbers of the relatives I'd traced who were still alive—a brother, sister, and several nephews and nieces. It was a very emotional moment for my mom when she called and caught up on the past forty years. I was thrilled that I was able to do this for my mom and that she was able to know her family again.

A few months later, I did take Mom on that dream trip to Japan, along with my father and my eight-year-old niece Sarah, who is half Japanese. We stayed in Osaka with Mom's sister Setsuko and her husband, Satoru. I soaked up all the stories of my mother's family, deepening my understanding of her. I was amazed at how my grandfather had raised thirteen children on his own after the death of my grandmother.

I asked my aunt, "Did he ever remarry?"

"No," she said, "and whenever someone asked him that question, he would always say, 'I married the only woman I was ever supposed to love.'"

From Osaka, we traveled on to Nagoya, Nara, and Kyoto. When I travel, I like to go off the beaten path, away from the tourists, to see where the locals go. My father, on the other hand, wanted to be right in the middle of every tourist in Japan. Everywhere we went, it seemed we were the Japanese version of the Griswolds.

It was a special trip, because for the first time I was able to experience how my mother had grown up, and to share it with the next generation through my niece.

But seeing my mother reconnect with her past stirred something unexpected in me. It reminded me of the missing piece of my own past: Who was my birth mother? What background had I come from? I'd already faced so many medical crises, and I wondered whether there were any hereditary medical problems that I should know about. I had spoken to private investigators, who all told me that it would be difficult to find the birth parent of a child who was born in a military hospital. Would I ever know where I came from? Would I ever be able to reconnect with my past?

☆   ☆   ☆

From the first year we met, Bruce always took special care to make sure I had a really nice holiday season, because the holidays also meant my birthday. He knew how I loved entertaining over the holidays. I always loved to cook, but at the holidays, I went overboard, cooking for more than a week beforehand. At Thanksgiving, Bruce would make the turkey (he knew to thaw it first by now!), and I would make everything else. He would start the night before by making the stuffing; he would use every dish, pan, and bowl in the kitchen, and after he was done, it would look like a tornado had come through. I loved that we were able to cook for this holiday together, and every year brought a new memory.

I had always been a fanatic for making the perfect holidays, wanting to create something magical that everyone would always remember. He noticed how I would get stressed if things didn't go as planned. Finally, one year he said to me, "You know, the people who love you won't care if things aren't perfect." In those few simple words, he had helped to make me a better person, and I enjoyed the holidays even more from that day on.

I had usually finished my shopping by Thanksgiving, so I wouldn't have to fight the crowds. I would hide my gifts throughout the house; some years, months after Christmas, I would find a gift or two stashed somewhere that I had forgotten. Because Bruce hated to shop, I would buy all the gifts he needed to give to his friends and family and would wrap them for him. Bruce would spend months figuring out what to give me; it would always be something that was thoughtful and that mattered to him. Whether it was a piece of jewelry he'd had custom made for me or a treasured keepsake from his past, he always found joy when giving it to me. He knew that he didn't have to buy me expensive gifts—it was the heartfelt gifts that mattered most to me. The letters he wrote expressing his love meant more to me than anything money could ever buy.

We would go out and buy a tree, and as I decorated the house, he would place the tree in the stand and place the ornaments on it—he always had a specific design in mind. After we both finished, I would make drinks, and we would lie in front of the fireplace listening to music for hours.

Every year we looked forward to the winters in Los Angeles, when it would finally get cool outside. We would lie on the sofa in front of the fire, and I would grab my music and play DJ for hours. There were many artists we both loved: Mark Knopfler, Tears for Fears, Tom Petty, Sarah McLachlan, Annie

Lennox, Muddy Waters, and all the jazz greats, such as Miles Davis, Chet Baker, and Louis Armstrong. I'm sure Bruce didn't like some of my music selections, but he rarely said anything—although he did draw the line at what he thought was sappy stuff, such as The Carpenters and Air Supply. We enjoyed being there in the moment, and he was even kind enough to put up with my singing.

We traveled to many places together, around the world and across the country. On September 10, 2001, we happened to be catching the subway under the World Trade Center. We had attended the US Open and were planning to stay one more day, but at the last moment something made us change our flight to leave that night. As we stood under the World Trade Center waiting for the train, something didn't seem right. I turned to Bruce and said, "I have this weird feeling that we will never be here again."

"What? Of course, we'll come back and do this again," he said, taking my hand.

We took a late flight back to Los Angeles. Bruce went right to bed, but I couldn't sleep, so I went downstairs to watch television. The moment I turned it on, the show I was watching was interrupted by a special report: the first tower had been hit. I then understood the meaning of the feeling I'd had while standing there that night under the World Trade Center.

I ran upstairs, woke Bruce up, turned the television on, and told him we were under attack. He said, "What are you talking about?" Just as he said that, the second building was hit by another plane. For the rest of the day, we lay in bed, glued

to the TV, thankful we had changed our flight back to LA to a day earlier.

Bruce's fiftieth birthday came, and I marked this milestone with a surprise birthday party at our house in Malibu. I made a list of all our friends. I called restaurants for catering, and a party supply company for the tables and chairs. And I had the cakes designed. All that was left was to coordinate how everything was going to be delivered and how to get him out of the house so I could put it all together. I decided the best way was to arrange for him to play tennis, a surefire way to get him out of the house. I set up a time for him to meet his friend Lou for a game.

Unbeknownst to me, Bruce decided to play tennis the night before and pulled a muscle in his back. I was worried he wouldn't make his tennis date for the next day, so I did everything—gave him massages, stretched out his back, and even made him take an Epsom salt bath, though he hated baths. He must have thought

I was going a bit overboard just for a pulled muscle. The next morning, he was still in bad shape, and I knew he wasn't going to be able to play. As the caterers started to arrive and set up, he came down the stairs to see what all of the commotion was about, and with a big smile on his face realized I had planned a party. When the guests arrived, he came down the stairs, we all yelled "Surprise!" and he hammed it up, pretending like a bad actor that he was surprised.

While we shared so much happiness, there were days Bruce would appear depressed, and I knew it was his memories of the past flaring up. His commitment and trust issues still hung over our relationship, no matter how much I assured him that I wasn't going anywhere. I would like to have married and started a family by now, but Bruce still didn't seem ready. At times I felt it would be easier to leave and not have to deal with the dysfunction of his former relationship, which continually seemed to envelop us. And after almost a decade together, things were about to come to a head.

For years, I had been relatively free of medical problems for the first time in my life. Then, one night in 2003, I was jolted awake at 3:00 AM by excruciating pain in my neck and the left side of my back, radiating down my arm to my fingertips. I tried to get up but found I was unable to lift my head off the pillow. I woke Bruce and tried to explain what was happening. He turned on the light and grabbed my cell phone to call my neurologist's number; then he realized what time it was. We lay there until 7:00 AM, and then Bruce called my doctor, who arranged for me to have an MRI at UCLA two hours later.

"We need to get you ready, sweetie," Bruce said when it was time to leave for the hospital.

"But how am I going to get up?" I said.

After thinking about it for a moment, Bruce came over and gently put his hand under my head and helped lift me up. On the drive to the hospital, I rested my head the best I could against the headrest. Thankfully I was the first patient of the morning and didn't have to sit in the waiting room.

The MRI showed a disk in my neck had exploded, most likely a long-term consequence of the car accident I'd been in eight years earlier. I was placed in a neck brace and told I was going to require surgery.

On the morning of the surgery, just before they wheeled me into the operating room, Bruce bent down and gave me a kiss. As I came to in recovery, Bruce was standing by my side, as he had many times before. I had made it through another surgery; I realized I had become far too familiar with the feeling of waking up in recovery at this point. The surgeon placed me in a hard collar.

"I want you to wear this until you come in to see me for your post-op appointment in a couple of weeks' time," he said. "And I want you to be very careful."

"We're scheduled to leave for France in a week. I can still go, can't I?" I said. Bruce and I had planned to go away for the holidays and my birthday.

"I don't recommend that you travel. If you were to fall, we won't be able to fix your disk again. You could be paralyzed," he said.

I took the surgeon's advice to heart, but I was determined that yet another medical issue was not going to ruin my plans. We flew to Paris and then traveled onward to a beautiful chateau, where a group of Bruce's friends had gathered to celebrate the holidays. After lunch the first day, Bruce and I walked through the property gathering chestnuts, with me all the while being careful not to fall. I didn't say anything to Bruce at the time, but I was a bit concerned that if something happened to me, we were far from home. I played it extra cautious.

On Christmas Day, everyone gathered at dinnertime to celebrate the holiday and my birthday. The evening started off well, with everybody chatting over dinner and enjoying themselves. But as the evening wore on, the tone started to change. The conversation had turned to how much it meant to me that my parents had adopted me, and this had led to me wanting to help others whenever I could. As they drained their wine glasses, I began to feel they were needling me. Then they became outright rude toward me, and one of the women said, "Who do you think you are, some saint?" I stood up from the table in tears, and as I walked back toward our room, I could hear them laughing at me.

Bruce soon followed and asked why I was so upset. I tried to explain the effect his friends' meanness had had on me—at a time when I was still in pain from surgery—but he just couldn't seem to understand where I was coming from. Perhaps he had also had too much to drink. I felt betrayed, let down, and unsupported.

"This is the worst birthday I've ever had," I sobbed. "I feel trapped here." All I wanted to do was get on a plane and go home. We had only two days left, though, so I did my best to keep quiet and make the most of our time left there.

At the airport in Paris waiting for our flight back to LA, we went to sit in the lounge, and as we both looked up at the television screen, we saw that CNN was reporting on fires in Malibu. We turned on our cell phones. Bruce's was filled with voicemails from Teresa, who was watching the house while we were away. I could hear the urgency in her voice as she left the messages. The TV coverage showed that the fire was just near our house, in an area that contained dry brush, and had spread up the hills quickly. At that moment, we had no idea what we were going to return to. Would we still have a house?

We had a driver pick us up at the airport, and as he drove us into Malibu, we could see charred hillsides and patches where the fire was still smoldering. As we turned into our street, we breathed sighs of relief: our house had been spared, while around us lay devastation. When we walked in, the house had the aroma of a barbecue on a hot summer day. I stopped and thought for a moment: this had been the worst trip of my entire life, but thank God the house had been spared.

As we settled back in after our trip, Bruce could tell I was angry about what had transpired in France, but he still couldn't understand why I was so upset that his friends had been cruel to me and that he had essentially sided with them rather than me. He always saw only the good in people; that was one of the things I loved about him. But he was very wrong about these friends. They weren't who he perceived them to be.

The disastrous trip to France had put a wedge between us, at a time when we were also going through the stress that came with my neck surgery. Again, under pressure, Bruce's commitment and trust issues reared up. Whatever happened to be going wrong for him, he blamed me for it. He became critical of me and short tempered, and soon we were back to having fights. I didn't like the person I was becoming, because I had allowed my resentment to change how I acted.

Too many times, I had found myself wishing he had never met this woman who'd hurt him. Even though he didn't have to deal with her any longer, she was still able to affect his life. I grew more and more frustrated, because I believed his progress had stalled on working through his trust issues. No matter how much love I showed him, he didn't seem convinced that I was there for him. It had been nine years. Was he ever going to heal from his past? I didn't know if I had anything left to give; I was exhausted.

And there was another reason I could no longer wait for Bruce to overcome his past: I wanted to start a family, and I was thirty-five years old.

One day during lunch, when I was trying to talk to him about what had happened in France, he tried to make small talk instead. I remained silent—until he said the wrong thing: "What is your problem?"

I had had enough and just let loose. If he wanted to know what the problem was, he was going to hear it. As he tried to walk away from me, I followed him, continuing the fight into the next room. Everything I had bottled up inside me came out. I screamed to him as loud as I could, "Please stop and look at me! I am not the woman who did this to you. I'm nothing like her and never will be! You say you love me more than you have ever loved anyone or anything, so prove it! I'm standing right before you, the girl who loves you with all her heart, and it's killing me that I'm paying for what someone else did to you. Please trust me—I want nothing more than to love you."

In the two weeks that followed, Bruce continually told me how much he loved me and that he didn't want me to leave, but I didn't feel that anything had substantially changed. I couldn't wait any longer. It was time to move on with my life while I was still young enough to have a family.

As I packed, wrapping up items of mine that had become tangled up with his things, it sunk in that this was really going to happen. When I had moved out for a few months to get a break years before, we both knew that it was going to be for a short period only and we would be back together, but this time felt different. Our possessions were symbols of how our lives came together nine years before. The day I'd moved in, I had seen so many things in our future together. We thought it would be forever. What had all that time meant, the nine years we had been together?

I fell apart as I packed and found myself remembering a scene from the movie I had watched the night before, *Pretty Woman*. At the end, the hero of the story went to the heroine's apartment to prove his undying love for her. Her wish had come true against all odds; her white knight had come to rescue her. I wished that Bruce would do the same: prove his love for me and tell me again that we were worth it. But in reality I knew that at this point in his life, he just couldn't understand exactly what he was losing. And I knew that if I stayed, he never would; nothing would change.

Moving day arrived, and he stayed in the bedroom while I had my stuff carried into the moving van. When it was time for me to leave, I went upstairs with a very heavy heart to say goodbye. It was apparent that Bruce had been crying. He reached for me and gave me a big hug and kiss and walked away in tears.

I was incredibly heartbroken. I wanted nothing more than to turn around, hold him, and be with him forever. I was moving back to the house we had lived in when we first met, the house where he had first told me he loved me. I cried the entire drive to the house and prayed that he could find a way to heal all the pain that he had gone through, and I prayed for the love we used to know. I just couldn't believe that we were really going our separate ways for good after all we had gone through to be together.

CHAPTER TEN

I t had been five years since I was diagnosed with cancer, and after a full-body scan to see if the cancer had returned, I was given the all-clear. My friends wanted to take me out that night to celebrate, and I agreed, even though I had to get up early the next morning. I had made plans with a friend to bike the LA Marathon, and we had to be downtown at 3:30 AM. The race was to signify my life without cancer, but never was it supposed to be the first day of the rest of my life without Bruce.

As I was preparing to leave the restaurant to go home after dinner, two men casually asked to join us. Chad sat across the table from me and introduced himself. He seemed to be a nice guy, and though my heart was still with Bruce, I was feeling some attraction toward him. It was getting late, and I had to leave. He asked me for my number, and I gave it to him.

A few days passed, and he called me from Miami. I said, "Ah, the old wait-a-few-days game. Don't want me to think you're too interested?" We both laughed and ended up speaking for more than an hour on the phone.

He asked me to go on a date with him when he returned to LA. At first I wanted to say no, because I felt I wasn't ready to start dating. Then I thought to myself: Bruce had been unable to set aside his fear of commitment, so maybe it was time for me to go on with my life. I accepted Chad's offer.

When he picked me up for our date, I was incredibly nervous because it still didn't feel right being with any man but Bruce. I asked, "Where are we going?"

"I can't tell you. It's a surprise—you have to trust me," he said. He drove me back to the restaurant where we had met. The surprise was that he had booked out the entire section of the restaurant for the two of us.

As much as I tried to fight having a nice time, I found myself liking Chad. It didn't hurt that he was handsome, Italian, and a lot of fun. I was very surprised how comfortable I was starting to feel with him.

He drove me home, and I invited him in for a drink. We sat on the sofa, and as I looked over at him, I started to tear up. This was where it had all begun for Bruce and me so many years before. I sat there wishing it were Bruce sitting there with me. I found myself wondering what his life would have been like if he had never met the person who'd hurt him years before. I had to remind myself that I had tried and given my heart fully to Bruce and that he may never be ready to accept it.

When Chad left, he gave me a kiss and asked me on another date. I agreed, but halfway through the date, I had a deep feeling of guilt, as if I were somehow cheating on Bruce. It soon got the best of me, and I train-wrecked the entire evening. I realized that I truly wasn't ready to date. All I wanted was to be with Bruce for the rest of my life. If only he could learn how to trust me and let go of what had been done to him in the past.

Bruce sent me letters in which he tried to get me to come back. It broke my heart to read them, but it also began the process of healing. As he spent time alone reflecting on our relationship, he was able to acknowledge my hurt, and he apologized. I have kept every single one of the letters he ever wrote to me. As I read them now, I can hear his voice clearly in my mind:

> You have been a true friend, and I have been on this sphere long enough now to realize what a rare and beautiful treasure that commodity is. I know that everything you have done has come from the fact that you cared for me, and I am profoundly sorry that I have been unable return your love and kindness in the manner in which you truly deserve.
>
> I let you down and abandoned you at times when you needed my support the most. When things became insane, so did I. I let my anger, fear, and

frustration get the better of me, and for that, please know I am disappointed in myself and will be forever sorry. It was never my intent to hurt you. At the relationship's darkest points, when I struck out in anger, you, on the other hand, never did.

Later Bruce would tell me that he spent his time at home, feeling depressed and having no interest in going out or dating. Then his older sister became terminally ill with cancer, and he went to San Francisco to be with her. It was hard on him to see her so sick and to watch her die. Helping her through her final days had a profound effect on his priorities. He wrote to me:

The agonizing and intensely emotional experience of caring for my sister through the last two months of her illness and her subsequent death were powerful reminders that our time on this planet is limited and how fast life really does pass us by.

I began to examine my life in an attempt to identify what it is that is truly important and meaningful. First and foremost is love of family, as you have always said. You are my family, and at the moment I am experiencing an overwhelming sense of loss. I've lost my sister, and I've lost my best friend. In many ways, I feel as if I have lost my entire family.

It turned out that my instincts about the dangers of having my Maltese, Nicky, with me after my cancer treatment were correct, even though the vet had assured me at the time that there was no risk. Nicky developed a persistent cough, and the vet found that the glands in his throat were enlarged. I felt devastated and guilty that I hadn't trusted my instincts. When he coughed at night, I would take him outside on the deck and let him lie on my chest in the cool air so he could fall asleep, and I would wake when the sun rose and take him back inside. I did this for weeks and was exhausted, but I was willing to do anything to make him more comfortable. His coughing got worse, and then his heart started to fail. He was suffering, and it became clear that the most compassionate thing I could do now for Nicky was to have him put to sleep. It tore me apart. He had been there to comfort me during a really hard time in my life, when I had brain surgery; now, just after I had been told I was cancer free, he had to leave me.

Bruce heard about Nicky's death and called to say he was sorry. "Melissa, I know how close you were to Nicky. Can I come and see you? I just want to comfort you if I can."

We had been apart for five months. I was reluctant to see him, because I was afraid to open up old wounds again. But we spoke a few more times on the phone, and I began to realize just how much I missed him. I invited him over, and as I opened the door, he reached for me, gave me a hug, and held me for the next few minutes. As he walked into the living room, I had flashbacks to the day I'd walked into that very same home nine years prior. We sat in the same place, where it had all begun, and a flood of emotions ran through me.

At that moment, I believe Bruce realized there was a window, and if he didn't take the opportunity to express how he was feeling, he might never get the chance again.

He said, "I have missed you, and I can't imagine my life without you. Will you please give us another chance? I promise you, everything you have ever wanted is right here."

"You know that I haven't changed my mind about starting a family, don't you, Bruce?" I said.

He nodded and said, "I have had a lot of sadness these past five months. I lost my sister to cancer, I lost you, and I can't bear to lose you again."

I was still having a hard time believing that he had really changed and was serious about committing to me fully, but I loved him more than I had ever loved anyone in my life. We both realized what we had lost when we were separated. He stayed the night. We lay, our bodies entangled, our lips joined, forgetting the world as it continued on, and dreaming of what the future held for us. There were no vows that held us together— only the love we felt that ran deep, and the knowledge that it couldn't be broken.

The next morning, when he woke, Bruce said, "I knew that I loved you, but it took losing you to realize just how much."

He stayed with me for the next three days. After that, we split our time between each other's houses, because we didn't want to be apart again. I cherish a letter that he wrote me during those days, because it reminds me of the joy of entering this new phase in our relationship:

> For the first time in nine years, the person I have never stopped loving is there in front of me, awake and alive. I cannot emphasize enough how powerful and exciting that is for me. After nine years of bottling my emotions and complete love for her away in a dark and lonely corner of my soul, I now have so much to tell her; so much to share with her. We are the only two souls who can truly understand what the other has been through.

> When memories of loved ones who are now gone from my life fill my heart with sadness and sorrow, I try to think, not of the emptiness left in their passing, but rather, the joy and love their souls brought to my life. I try to think, not of what is now lost to me, but rather, what currently brings joy and happiness into my life. Most of all . . . I think of you.

It's amazing, when you love someone deeply, how much you can remember; I have never forgotten a moment of our time together and the words we spoke, good and bad. The good times reminded us how much the hardest days were worth it. Every relationship goes through rough spots at one time or another;

it's the love you feel inside for each other that keeps you fighting to save the relationship. As the saying goes, "The couples that are meant to be are the ones who go through everything that is meant to tear them apart, and come out even stronger."

There was this struggle in our lives, but there was always something stronger between us; when it seemed something would tear us apart, that strength pulled us back together. I was cautious about opening my heart again, in case Bruce was not really ready. Was our love strong enough to get through all the obstacles life would put in front of us? I didn't have the answer to that question, but I did know that, if I didn't give it this one last try, I might never know what could have been.

CHAPTER ELEVEN

It was Christmas Eve, and while Bruce and I were separated, I had made plans to visit my friend Claudia, who I had met through my business, in San Francisco for my birthday and Christmas. As we pulled up to the airport in LA and I gave Bruce a kiss, I had second thoughts about going, because I didn't want to be away from him. But I knew it would be good for us to reflect on what we had just experienced and that I would see him in a few days.

As soon as I arrived, Claudia and I started running around the city, shopping and eating at restaurants. We returned to her apartment late in the day with handfuls of shopping bags. I had done all of my Christmas shopping in one day and had purchased gifts for Bruce that I knew he would love: a suede blazer, leather driving moccasins, some beautiful dress shirts, and a silver flask. We were going out for dinner and dancing with Claudia's friends that night.

"I'm just going to go get ready, okay?" I called to Claudia as I laid all my bags down on the floor in the dining room and sat down a couple of feet from the Christmas tree. I saw a flash of red. It took a second for my mind to work out what my eyes were seeing. "The Christmas tree, it's on fire!"

In a matter of seconds, the tree was completely engulfed in flames, burning like a Roman torch. The fire spread through the room very quickly. Claudia immediately tried calling 911, but the line was busy—later we found out that there was a brown out. She made her way outside, down a flight of stairs, to see if she could get cell-phone reception.

I stood there in the middle of the room for a moment, mesmerized, experiencing no fear as I watched the fire unfurl over my head like a wave of silk. I experienced no fear; I felt as if something were protecting me. A sense of calm settled over me, as if I was being guided. As I made my way to the back door, I realized I had forgotten my purse. By this time, the room was filled with flames and smoke, but I knew I had to get back to Los Angeles and that everything was in that purse, so I ran back. Just as I got to my purse, the ceiling started to come down. As I crouched on the floor and reached for my purse, pieces of the burning ceiling fell on my hand.

I was barefoot, and there were embers everywhere; I crawled on my hands and knees to the back door. As I made my way down the stairs, the heat from the fire blew out the window above me. The door at the bottom of the stairs, which led outside, was stuck. As the fire raged in the apartment, I struggled with the door for a few minutes. Finally, I was able to push it open and make my way to the street, and it began to rain. Claudia was standing there, anxiously waiting for me to come out. She was in complete shock that her house was engulfed in flames, though she was relieved that I'd made it out alive. We gave one another a hug, and I told her it was going to be okay. Minutes later, the rest of the windows blew out from the heat. The fire trucks arrived and started putting out the fire.

My first thought was to call Bruce; I needed to hear his voice. I was in tears, and he could barely understand me. I remember hearing the fear in his voice that he could have lost me. When I hung up the phone, I just wanted to be home with him. It was Christmas—why weren't we together? What if I hadn't made it out alive? We would have never seen each other again.

People came up to me and Claudia, offering their help. "What I really need is to get this hand seen by a doctor," I said. My hand had been badly burned when part of the ceiling collapsed on me. The Red Cross arrived and immediately began offering assistance.

"There's a burn clinic just two blocks away," one of the passersby said.

Claudia and I got directions and began walking. That's when I realized my feet had been burned, too, on my way to the back door. A man came out of his home and, seeing that I was barefoot, handed me a pair of men's size 11 brown wingtip shoes. Given that I wear a women's 8½ shoe, it was pretty interesting trying to walk in the wingtips, but I was just thankful for the man's kindness. At the burn center, which fortunately turned out to be one of the top burn facilities in the country, I was treated for second- and third-degree burns and released. I was in a lot of pain, but probably more stunned by what Claudia and I had just gone through.

I called a friend who managed a hotel down the street and explained what had happened. She arranged a room for us to stay in, but I don't think she was prepared for what was coming to greet her. There I stood at the front desk, wearing a white t-shirt and jeans that were completely covered in soot, and men's size 11 brown wingtip shoes. We both smelled like a barbecue. I will never forget the faces of all the snooty people in the lobby and bar looking down their noses at us, as if they had just allowed two homeless people to stay in the hotel.

The first thing I did when we got to our room was to take a shower and wash all the soot from my body and hair. As we lay there in our beds that night, all we could say was, "It just doesn't seem real, does it?" We were both in shock. I pictured the scene in my mind, over and over again, of the wave of fire rushing across the ceiling above my head. It was sinking in how lucky we were to have made it out alive, and maybe just how crazy I had been to go back for my purse as the apartment was burning. I once again wondered why I had been spared. What was my purpose?

We didn't get very much sleep that night. When we woke on Christmas morning, we put our stinky, smoky clothes back on, and Claudia laughed as I put on the very large wingtip shoes.

We walked over to her building, and all that was left of Claudia's apartment was a pile of charred remains that the firemen had shoveled onto the sidewalk. We began to sift through the rubble, and within a few minutes, Claudia had stumbled across a pile of photos that seemed untouched by the fire and in perfect condition. She snatched them up, eagerly started sifting through them—and realized they were of her ex-husband. She threw them back in the pile, and we started laughing hysterically. The people walking by must have thought we were insane.

Peeking through the burned-out wreckage were my favorite brown suede boots, but as I pulled them out, I saw that the toes had curled up, like genie shoes. I started finding bits and pieces of the gifts that I had purchased for Bruce for Christmas—fragments of suede from the jacket, the sleeve of one of the dress shirts.

As we searched for anything that may have survived the fire, people came up to us to show their support. When they found out it was my birthday, they offered me money to buy food, and a few people invited us to their home for Christmas dinner. My heart melted with appreciation. At that moment, I realized I had just been given the greatest birthday and Christmas gift of my life; their generosity represented the true meaning of the holiday. I thanked each and every one of them for their kindness.

Remembering that she had a few things in storage in the basement of her building, Claudia went downstairs. Minutes later, she came back wearing a pair of black, high-heeled, lace-up granny boots. Together with Dolce and Gabbana jeans and a cashmere top, they made for a bizarre outfit. She was usually so meticulously put together and stylish. Stunned, I couldn't help but burst out laughing, and that set her off laughing, too. While many people would have been devastated and depressed after losing their home, Claudia was a trooper, and she was doing a good job of staying positive. Laughing seemed to be helping make things bearable for her.

Clearly, we needed clothes, but the only store nearby that was open on Christmas Day was a Walgreens down the street. We walked there to see if there was anything we could buy to get us through till the next day, when all the stores would open for the big after-Christmas sales. The only clothes they had were black sweat pants with a white stripe down the side, and San Francisco t-shirts and fleece sweatshirts for the tourists. We walked back to the hotel and changed into our new clothes.

I thought we were going to die from laughter as we both looked in the mirror. There Claudia stood, wearing her tourist outfit, the bottom of her sweat pants sitting about four inches above her ankles, which meant you could see her high-heel granny boots. I didn't look any better, wearing the same outfit, only with my size 11 brown wingtip shoes.

"Come on, let me take a photo. It would make the best holiday card!" I joked.

"No way!" she shot back.

We went down to the hotel restaurant, picked up food, went back to our room, and Claudia spent the rest of the day making phone calls to her insurance, cell-phone, and credit-card companies.

The next morning, there we were back in our tourist outfits, going shopping for new clothes and replacing all of Bruce's gifts that had been lost in the fire. We laughed so hard we were in tears as we walked down the block. We went to Union Square, where the poshest stores are. As we would walk into a store, the staff would look at us the same way the staff looked at Julia Roberts' character in *Pretty Woman* when she went shopping on Rodeo Drive in her hooker outfit. There I stood with my Platinum card, and no one would help us.

I was sad to leave my friend behind to have to deal with all the mess on her own, but my flight was leaving later that day. When I returned home, I was greeted by the warmest embrace, and Bruce said, "I don't know what I would have done if I had lost you."

☆　☆　☆

Two weeks after the fire, I found out that I was pregnant. I could hardly contain my excitement that day as I waited to share the good news with Bruce. When he came home from playing tennis and sat down next to me, I was ready to burst. He had no idea what I was about to tell him, but from the look on his face I could tell he was intrigued to find out what could possibly have made me so excited. I couldn't hold it in any longer. Before he had a chance to say anything, I said, "I have something to share with you: We are pregnant!"

At first, Bruce appeared stunned, and then as my news sank in, a smile spread across his face, and his eyes lit up with happiness. He leaned in and kissed me.

"This is the beginning of the rest of our lives together," he said.

"Everything we've been through to get to this point . . . it was all worth it," I replied.

For the first time in a long time, I allowed myself to feel joy, because all of my dreams were really going to come true. The only man I had ever truly loved was back in my life, we had a baby on the way, and we were planning the rest of our lives together. We couldn't have been happier.

Bruce came to every doctor's appointment with me. I will never forget the look in his eyes the day of my first ultrasound. "That's our baby," he said, overawed.

On the ride home, he said, "For the first time in my life, I have a chance to really be happy and to have the family I always wanted."

I spent the days planning the baby's room and buying maternity clothes. At night in bed, Bruce would lie next to me, place his hand on my stomach, and say he was pretty sure it was going to be a boy. It was what he always wanted.

At my next checkup, when I was more than three and a half months pregnant, the doctor performing the ultrasound stopped what he was doing and looked at me. He gave us the news that we thought we would never hear again: "I'm sorry. The baby didn't make it."

I was completely inconsolable. We left the office in disbelief; our world had once again been shattered.

"What did I ever do to deserve my life?" I asked Bruce on the drive home.

I cried the entire night, hoping I could fall asleep and wake in the morning to find it had all been just a dream. Bruce was completely devastated, too. He rolled over and held me and said, "I am so sorry. Maybe this isn't the right time, but we can try again."

"I don't think I can go through this again," I said, through my sobs. "Maybe there is a reason I am not supposed to have children."

CHAPTER TWELVE

We needed to get away from LA and spend some time healing together, so I planned a trip to the Far East that would be full of surprises for Bruce and hopefully bring some happiness back into our lives. I arranged everything, and all he knew was that we were going to the Far East, but not where and why.

When we arrived in Singapore, as we entered the hotel lobby, we were greeted by his old high school friends, whom I had arranged to fly in from Japan to be with him. They spent the evening telling stories about their days in school. I sat back and listened and could see Bruce was happy.

We had three days in Singapore, staying at the Four Seasons Hotel overlooking the park. We walked through the park, had lunch, went shopping, enjoyed the city—and made sure not to throw gum on the street! We would wake early, get dressed, and go to the restaurant for breakfast; Bruce kept mentioning how much he had missed the service that you get in the Far East. I was so impressed that he was waking early that I barely even noticed the service.

We traveled on to the Philippines, back to where Bruce had been born and had spent the first thirteen years of his life. I had a special surprise for him: he was going to go back to the house where he had grown up. I had arranged it with one of the partners in the shipping company where his father worked, who had purchased the house from his parents when they moved to Tokyo. Bruce was like a kid in a candy store, and I got to share his joy as he walked through the house reliving old memories. "Not much has changed in my bedroom, but it's hard to believe how I fit in there," he said. I believe it's something we have probably all thought when we looked through an adult's eyes at our first bedroom.

We went to lunch in the city with one of Bruce's friends, who brought one of his dogs. He had three bichons, but this one was his favorite. It was a nice restaurant, and apparently he ate there often, because the waiters basically rolled out the red carpet for us. As we sat down, I looked to my right, and there seated in the next chair was the dog—he had his own place at the table! We ordered, and when the food arrived, so did a plate for the dog. I couldn't believe it. A few minutes later, a group of men sat down at the table beside ours and greeted Bruce's friend, whom they knew. Bruce's friend leaned over to Bruce and said, "See the guy on the far right? He is the health inspector." We all laughed, and it became clear how powerful Bruce's friend was if the health inspector was prepared to turn a blind eye to the dog sitting at our table. During lunch, I could see how happy it made Bruce to be able to reminisce about his childhood.

We drove through Manila, and Bruce told me stories as we passed places that he remembered as a child. As we came to a traffic light near his home, he told me that when he was a kid, there wasn't a traffic light. There was a guy sitting on a chair, and when people got to the light, he would lift a lever to change the color of the light. The traffic in Manila was awfully congested, and Bruce was having a hard time believing so much had changed and so many years had passed since he had been home.

We had a great time in the Philippines, traveling to areas Bruce had never been to as a child, and I was glad that we could experience them for the first time together. He told me how sad he was to have to leave. I said, "Don't worry—we'll go back again one day." But as I spoke, I remember getting a strange feeling that we wouldn't return.

We boarded a flight and traveled to Hong Kong, which was still under British rule at the time. I continued to make sure that Bruce didn't know where we would be going until we were leaving for our destination. It became a game for him, and he kept trying to guess where we would be staying. When we arrived at the hotel and he realized we were staying at The Peninsula, I'm sure he knew why I had chosen it. That was an easy one, because he had told me many stories of time spent at the Peninsula as a child. I had arranged for us to stay in a suite overlooking the harbor. People had said it was the most stunning city view in the world. They were correct, and we had a bird's-eye view every night right from our room.

We would wake in the morning, walk down to the lobby to have breakfast, and then go for a walk along the water. As we walked through the city, he told me stories of when he would travel to Hong Kong as a child with his mother, and how she would make him go shopping. When we first met, if I wanted him to go shopping with me, he would always say, "I hate to shop—please don't make me go." I would always laugh, because I could picture him being dragged into the stores as a little boy who had no choice. So I never made him go shopping with me. He was spoiled; I bought all of his clothes and everything he would ever need.

As we sat in the lobby of The Peninsula, Bruce told me that when he was a little boy, his mom would drag him to have tea with all the old ladies. He looked so cute when he told me these stories, as he pictured those moments in his mind. He was fortunate as a child to have experienced such travel, and I always felt our lives were enriched by each other's experiences.

Soon after we returned from our trip to the Far East, we were sitting at the kitchen table, and I received a call from a friend in the hotel business, asking if I would be interested in working on a hotel on the island of Bora Bora, near Tahiti.

By now, I had been working with hotels for almost twenty years. "I'm just not sure I want to work on another project," I said to Bruce when I got off the phone.

"Well, you know, if you want to retire from the hotel business, Bora Bora would be the perfect place to do it," he said.

The man had a point. I got excited when I realized that I could take Bruce along and make it a truly memorable trip. I loved to surprise Bruce, and since this was going to be the last hotel project I would ever work on, this would be my best surprise yet. I started planning before we even left the United States, sending emails to the manager of the hotel and shopping for things I could take with me in my suitcase that would help me pull off my surprise. All the while, he had no clue what I was up to.

We flew to Tahiti and made our way to Bora Bora by boat. As we docked at the resort, we marveled at the water, which was the most beautiful turquoise color. I had arranged for us to stay in a large luxurious hut sitting on stilts over the sparkling ocean. I attended a few meetings, and luckily that lasted only two days. Now I would have the rest of the time on the island to just have fun with Bruce and plan my surprise.

While Bruce slept in every morning, I would wake as the sun rose and dive off a platform from our room into the warm ocean. Living in Los Angeles, where the water is freezing cold, getting into the ocean isn't an option, so to be able to do this was heaven for me. I took every opportunity I could to be in the water. When Bruce got up, we would start our day together kayaking, swimming, and snorkeling. We would usually end our day by having a glass of wine, sitting on the deck, watching the most beautiful sunsets on earth. Every evening seemed to bring an even more beautiful sunset than the one before.

On Valentine's Day morning, I woke and turned toward Bruce to watch him sleep. As the sun rose, it cast a beautiful glow on his face. There was a softness and peace in that moment, and I didn't want it to end.

I had let Bruce think that I had arranged for us to have dinner in the restaurant that night. Little did he know I had something much grander planned. That afternoon, I told him I had to go to the front desk to handle a few things and that I would be back in a bit. In advance, I had reserved the entire beach just for the two of us and had it roped off. Now I gathered supplies from housekeeping, covered the beach with white sheets, and arranged twenty pillows. Using red silk rose petals I'd brought from LA, I created a trail for him to follow. I placed seventy-five votive candles in the sand and lit them as the time was nearing for him to arrive. The front desk sent a golf cart to pick him up and told him that I'd asked for them to pick him up and bring him to the restaurant.

I'm sure he was wondering where on earth they were taking him when they passed the restaurant, but as he arrived and began to follow the trail of rose petals, he could see me lying on the sheets on the sand. He walked toward me just as the sun was setting, wearing a white linen shirt and tan linen pants. My heart started to beat faster out of excitement. He lay next to me and said, "I can't believe you did all of this for me!" The waiters arrived with champagne, and soon a five-course meal was served. We fed each other dessert and blew out all of the votive candles, and after we made love, we walked back to the room under the light of the moon.

The following Valentine's Day, not wanting to be outdone, Bruce planned a surprise evening of his own for me. While I was out shopping and having lunch with friends, I received a call from him asking if I could meet him at the house around 6:00 PM. He told me he wanted to take me to this new restaurant in town, the Gnu Gnu Macambo Lounge. I had never heard of it, but it sounded interesting.

I arrived home at 6:00 PM as he requested, and as I entered through the kitchen door, I was greeted with the sight of more than ten dozen roses sitting in vases. Yes, I counted them, because I couldn't believe he had purchased so many. The lights were dim, and I could tell he was up to something. I followed a trail of rose petals that he had laid, which led me to one of our guest bedrooms. As I opened the door, he was standing there with one rose in his hand, and a great big smile. He handed me the rose, gave me a kiss, and said, "Welcome to the Gnu Gnu Macambo Lounge." He had removed everything from the room and brought in the Indonesian coffee table from the living room, and then piled about ten large Moroccan pillows that he had bought against the wall in front of the table for us to sit on. He brought in tables from around the house to place candles on, making sure they were different heights so it would look nicer. He closed the curtains, and when I walked in, the entire room was a glow of candles. There were as many as I had placed on the beach in Bora Bora—I thought he was going to burn down the house!

He asked me to have a seat on one of the cushions, poured a glass of champagne for each of us, and sat down beside me.

"I can't believe you were able to pull off this surprise without me knowing!" I said, and we both laughed. "I love the name of your new restaurant, by the way."

"If you'll just excuse me for a moment," he said, standing up. As I went to get up to help him, he said, "Stay here—this night is all for you. I'll be right back." He returned with a large tray: he had prepared a delicious dinner for us. When we had finished everything on our plates, he once again excused himself, and a few minutes later returned with dessert. He fed me strawberries that he had hand dipped in chocolate.

He reached over to give me a kiss, and I began to cry, wondering how I could have been so lucky to have met this man who wanted to do such special things for me. As we lay there, he had the perfect music playing—Billie Holiday, Nina Simone, Van Morrison. We were so comfortable we fell asleep in each other's arms. The next morning, I woke before him, went into the kitchen, and made him his favorite breakfast, French toast made with brioche, and a double-shot cappuccino. We spent the rest of the day in bed overlooking the ocean.

☆   ☆   ☆

We were still splitting our time between our two houses, and we were getting tired of it. Bruce's father had died years before, and up until recently, his mother had been living alone in the big beach house in Hawaii that had been the family's winter home when Bruce was a child. When her health declined, she'd moved into an assisted-living facility, and now she had passed away. The family had decided to sell the house, so we traveled to Hawaii to sort through Bruce's mother's things to get the house ready for sale.

As we were packing one day, Bruce took me by the arm and stopped me. "I don't want to sell the house. It's the last thing I have left of my family," he said. "I want to buy it and fix it up. Will you move here with me for a while and help me restore the house?"

I gazed around the room. The house hadn't been properly maintained for years, and the ocean salt had taken its toll. Every inch of the place needed work. "I don't know, Bruce. There's about six months worth of work here," I said. I didn't know if had the energy for the project, but I could see it was important to him. "Okay, yes!" I said. The look on his face when I agreed was priceless.

Renovating the house in Hawaii would mean putting my plans for a new career on hold. Since getting out of the hotel business, I had come up with an idea that took me back to my early days in LA, when I'd started working in the hair-care product industry. I had put together a business plan and begun researching laboratories and packaging manufacturers for my own product line, and had come up with a name for my company and contacted an attorney to trademark the brand. I was excited to get started, but all of that could wait.

Bruce purchased the house, and we returned to Los Angeles and packed our things, because we were going to be living in Hawaii for the next six months.

The day we arrived, Bruce reached up to the plumeria tree in the garden and picked one of the fragrant yellow-and-white flowers. He gently placed it behind my ear and said, "Welcome to our new home." He opened the door, and as I entered and looked around, I thought, what in the heck did I get myself into? There was even more work to do than I had remembered.

The house was a complete mess. There was no room that we felt comfortable sleeping in, so we bought a blow-up mattress, sheets, and pillows, and slept on the lanai. I got up in the middle of the night to get a drink, and when I turned on the kitchen light, ten feet away on the wall was the biggest spider I had ever seen. I'm pretty sure I woke half of the neighborhood. Bruce came running into the kitchen naked, thinking someone had attacked me. He laughed and said, "Good Lord, it won't bother you, come back to bed." Within minutes, he was fast asleep. I believe I slept with one eye open the rest of the night.

The next morning, I discovered that Bruce was no stranger to the creepy-crawlies in the old house. Not long after we'd met, he'd gone to visit his mother, and for privacy, he took the room that was at the farthest end of the house, which hadn't been occupied in years.

"The bed was buried in junk, so I cleared everything off it and tried to make it as comfortable as I could. Then I unpacked and went to have a shower," he said. "I'd been standing in the shower for a few minutes, letting the nice warm water trickle over me, when I suddenly realized that water doesn't trickle *up* your legs. I looked down . . . and there were hundreds of roaches running out of the drain and crawling up my legs."

I couldn't help but shudder. "Oh, my God! What did you do?"

"I brushed them off and ran out of the shower. I slammed that door behind me so fast. Those roaches were the size of Volkswagens!"

Apparently, as no one had used that shower in years, the roaches had decided to nest in the pipes.

"Hmm, are you sure this is the best time to tell me this story? I mean, I did just experience a spider the size of a Mack truck!"

"Those spiders really are harmless," he assured me.

"I don't care whether they're harmless or not. It was hairy and very, very large, like a tarantula. I don't want anything to do with them," I said. I was ready to check into a hotel until the house was finished. But I decided to stick it out, and we actually had a lot of fun sleeping on the lanai. Neither of us wore clothes to sleep, so when we woke in the morning, we would each grab a towel and carefully wrap ourselves before standing, hoping that no one would see us from the beach. After a few days, Bruce said, "The hell with it," and would walk buck naked into the house. He had a really nice body, so I never minded; if the neighbors saw, they wouldn't have, either.

We wasted no time and got started on the renovations. I walked into the kitchen, grabbed a sledgehammer, and leveled this old desk that was sitting right in the entrance to the kitchen.

Realizing I was going to demolish everything old in sight, he made a phone call and asked Milton, a contractor he'd heard good things about, to come over. Bruce had a list of things to do around the house, but each time he asked Milton if he could do a particular job, Milton would answer, "No." It seemed that Milton wouldn't be able to help us with most of the construction that needed to be done to the house, but he agreed to come back the following morning to start work on the things he could do. In the next few days, we started to learn that Milton hadn't answered so truthfully to Bruce's questions—he had probably been afraid of committing to the giant job that lay ahead of us. We soon found there was nothing Milton couldn't do. He could have torn the entire house down and rebuilt it on his own.

We were still putting the final touches on the house right up until the moment the cab came to take us to the airport at the end of our six months. As we shut the door, Bruce said, "I wish we didn't have to leave." Even though fixing the house had been a lot of hard work, we'd found a peace in Hawaii that we didn't have in Los Angeles. We made a decision: when I turned fifty, we were going to move to Hawaii permanently and grow old together.

CHAPTER THIRTEEN

On my thirty-seventh birthday, Bruce and I were sitting by the Christmas tree, having just finished opening all our presents to each other.

"Sweetie, there's one more present. I was waiting to give you this one last," he said, handing me a card.

I opened it, and as I read what he had written inside, I broke down in tears:

Dearest Melissa,

The greatest gift I could think of to give you this Christmas was to reunite you with your birth mother. I wanted it to be a surprise, but I was unable to proceed without your assistance, so please accept this gift as a small token of my

love for you, and we will find your birth mother
together.

Once the holidays had passed, we immediately started looking for an investigator in the Washington, D.C. area. Within a
few hours, I was able to find an investigator, Donna, who in the
past had worked for an adoption agency. Bruce hired her, and
the following day, we boarded a plane to Hawaii for a few weeks.

As soon as we arrived at the house, I immediately received a
call. She had found my birth mother, whose name was Marilyn.
I couldn't believe how quickly she had done it, after investigators
in the past had warned me about the difficulties of tracing a
mother in the military hospital system.

"Would you like to speak with her?" Donna asked. I was
stunned. Everything was moving so fast. "How about if I have
her call you?"

"Yes, please do," I answered. It would give me a bit of time
to prepare to speak with her.

I ran down to the beach and shared my news with Bruce,
and about an hour later, I received the call. I am not sure if I
could ever explain what it feels like to speak for the first time
with someone who is in reality a stranger but who at the same
time you feel that you should know because you are connected
to them biologically. Her voice was raspy, like a smoker's, and
at first she sounded nervous.

Telling me all about her life, she gradually began to relax. She
was from Fort Lauderdale, Florida, and her father was a retired

Navy cook, while her Mom was a homemaker. When she found out that she was pregnant at the age of seventeen and a high school student, she had gone to live with her aunt and uncle near Andrews Air Force Base for eight months, until I was delivered. The day I was born, the nurses let her hold me, even though they weren't supposed to. When I was in her arms, she wanted to change her mind and keep me. Then she thought it through: she wanted me to have a good life, and she was too young to provide that. For years after, she felt guilty for giving me up.

"Have you had a good life, Melissa?" she asked me hopefully.

"The best," I assured her. "I was given to the most caring people, who showed me love and taught me to be a good person."

She exhaled deeply, and I could tell she was relieved. "Do you have any other questions for me? she offered.

There were two questions that I had prepared almost my entire life to ask. "What time was I born?" I asked her first.

"Ten thirty-five a.m. on Christmas Day," she replied. Finally knowing what time I came into this world helped to give me a sense of completion.

"There is just one more question," I said. "Were there any medical problems in your family?"

"Nothing much, no cancer or anything like that. Most of my relatives have lived very long lives," she said, and it came as a relief to me.

"Are you sure that's all you want to know?" she asked.

"Thank you, but those were the two questions I've always wanted to ask you. The rest I can find out in time."

My birth mother went on to tell me that she now lived in New York. She had married and had a daughter eighteen years after I was born. Three years later, she delivered another daughter on Christmas Day, two minutes after I had been born. She had taken it as a sign from God that she had been forgiven for giving me up years before.

I agreed and said, "Maybe the clock was wrong by two minutes in the delivery room, and we were born at the same time." I could tell she was a kind, caring person, and she didn't need to beat herself up any longer. She had given me an amazing gift, and I had a good life. I was exactly where I was supposed to be, because she had graciously given me up so that I could have the kind of life she wasn't capable of giving me at the time.

Months later, I received a call from my half-sister Ashley, who was born twenty-one years after me and lived in New York. She was going to be in Los Angeles and wanted to meet. We made plans to go to a local hotel on the beach, and there we sat for the first time, chatting as if we had known each other for years. I began regularly speaking on the phone to my other half-sister, Angel, who was born eighteen years after me and lived in Philadelphia. We soon learned we have many things in common: we are both very health oriented, have a passion for cooking, love crafts, and are very organized.

It has been wonderful to connect with my birth mother and half-sisters, but it does still bother me that I don't know who my biological father is and that there is a man out there who has a daughter he knows nothing about.

☆ ☆ ☆

Bruce and I loved to travel the world, but one day he truly surprised me when out of the blue he said he wanted to take me to Venice, Italy. For years I had told him that Italy was the one place I held sacred, the one place where I would go only when I was married.

"If all the years we have been together and what we have been through don't constitute being married, I don't know what does," he joked when I brought it up again.

I laughed and said, "Okay, then—I guess we're going to Italy."

He booked the airline tickets, and I made a call to get connected to stay at a beautiful hotel on the water. After we had arrived at the hotel by water taxi and dropped our bags in our room, we walked through the city until we found a café. We sat and ordered coffee, and I noticed an elderly couple sitting next to us. Bruce knew I was going to have a conversation with them—anyone who knows me knows that if there is someone within a twenty-foot radius, I will be acquainted with them before leaving. They were from Nebraska, and for a few minutes, we shared stories. Then the lady said, "I hope you two have a long, happy marriage like we've had."

Bruce smiled and said, "I hope so, too."

After we left the café, we turned to walk down an alley. There was a bakery, and the front window caught Bruce's eye, because the baker had a talent for making bread in the shape of people's faces. The way they were displayed in the window made for a great photo, and Bruce didn't miss the opportunity to take the shot. Each day of the trip, he spent hours taking photographs throughout the city. Some days we would go back to the same location a couple of times, waiting for the perfect light, so he could get the perfect shot. I was pleasantly surprised, because I hadn't seen him do that in years. It was usually me taking the photos. When we traveled, if I asked him to take photos, he would always laugh and say, "I only take photos when I'm getting paid."

After we returned to Los Angeles, I would catch him on the computer, touching up the photos from Venice. I was curious about what he planned on doing with them, but he would never tell me.

That Christmas, as I opened my birthday gift, I finally realized what he'd been planning. The reason he had taken all those photos in Italy was as a gift for me. He had made a hard-bound book of our trip, with prints of his photos interspersed with his words of love and affection translated into Italian.

As I thumbed through the book and looked at the beautiful images, I couldn't help but stop at the photos of me and feel sad. I was sick during that trip, as I'd been having issues with my immune system and digestion that led to my whole body, including my face, being swollen—to the point where I was unrecognizable to people who knew me. I was reminded of how many photos he had taken of me over the years that chronicled one illness after another. Without thinking, I expressed how upset I was that he had included the photos of me in the book, as if he was intentionally trying to hurt me. Deep down, I knew he wasn't. I was overreacting. Later, I apologized and told him that the reason I had been upset was that I wanted him to see me only as beautiful. He said, "I could never see you as anything but."

I felt terrible that I had hurt him that day, when he was only trying to do something special and kind for me. As I look through the book today, the images that had upset me don't bother me anymore. I have come to accept that there were times in my life that I didn't feel beautiful, yet all along, his feelings stayed constant.

From the moment we purchased the house in Malibu, I'd never had a good feeling there. It always had a bad energy. Our relationship had gone through hell in that house, and we both felt it was time to simplify our lives. We undertook a complete renovation in preparation to sell. It was an incredibly stressful time for the both of us, but when the renovation was complete, we were able to sell the house and move into our home in Santa Monica—the house where we first met. We planned on being there for a while, so we thought we should make some changes to it, too. I was very hesitant to get involved in another renovation, but the house was small, and we needed a guesthouse.

Six months later, the house was finished, and we jumped on a plane to Hawaii to get some rest.

As with every time before, when we stepped off the plane, we got the feeling that we were home. We could leave the stress of Los Angeles behind; this was our escape from it all. We would always take the same flight, which arrived in Hawaii at 11:00 am, and by the time we got to the house, we were starved. Bruce had a routine: he would attach the battery to the car, get gas, wash the car, buy me flowers, and return to the house. We would walk over to a local restaurant and get a Hawaiian staple: plate lunch. I'd crave it as soon as I walked off the plane, sometimes even while the plane was in flight. We always ordered barbecue teriyaki chicken, which came with rice and macaroni salad. My first time ordering it years ago, I thought, "What an odd combination," but, strangely, it works.

Every Sunday morning we would take a drive around the island, because Bruce loved the color of the water on the other side, which I could never understand. Our side had beautiful turquoise water, while on the other side it was a deep cobalt blue. It was pretty, but to me it was too similar to California's ocean. On our way home, we would stop at Dave's Ice Cream shop to get our favorite flavors, green tea and coffee. We would buy enough for a week, but somehow it never lasted more than two days. It was a good thing they weren't closer to the house, or we would have needed to go on a diet every time we returned to Los Angeles.

I remember the darkness of the sky in Hawaii at night. Bruce would grab a blanket, and we would lie on the beach. The sky was as black as you could ever imagine; we weren't used to it, living in Los Angeles with all the city lights. He would put his arm around me, and we would lie there for hours, watching for shooting stars. He would say, "This is our Shangri-la," knowing that was my favorite Mark Knopfler song. Whenever we heard it being played, it reminded us both of our times together in Hawaii.

We always felt sad when we had to leave, but this time when we returned to Los Angeles, I could see that Bruce had become more depressed than ever about having to leave. He normally never woke before me, but when I woke the next morning, he was sitting there bright-eyed, waiting for me to open my eyes. He looked at me and said, "Let's move to Hawaii. I don't have anything keeping me in LA, and we always say we hate to leave. Now we won't have to."

I wasn't completely awake yet and said, "Okay." It was an off-the-cuff response. Was I ready for such a quiet lifestyle? I was only forty-two years old.

That night during dinner, Bruce said, "I spoke to an agent in Hawaii today, and they're interested in representing me. I want to start doing photography again."

"Oh Bruce, I'm so excited! You're going to be doing what you love again!" I said.

"And you know, there's nothing to stop you from launching your business there," he replied. He was right. Hawaii might have a quieter lifestyle, but I could finally get my hair-care product line off the ground. It had taken me two years to build my business, and it was almost ready to be launched. It was funny: we were moving to paradise, and we would probably be busier living there than in Los Angeles.

I started packing the house. In two months, the moving trucks would arrive, and there were so many things to take care of. At first, Bruce wanted to sell the Santa Monica house, because he wasn't planning on returning, but I convinced him to keep it just in case we ever got island fever and wanted to return to LA.

A few days later, we were lying in bed, and Bruce rolled over and said, "I'm glad we're moving to Hawaii, and you know how much I love you. Will you marry me?"

We had been together so many years that we knew it was for life, but for some reason, he had decided that it was finally time to make it official. I said, "Yes" and was then surprised to find out that he must have been thinking about our wedding for quite some time. He had planned out the ceremony, and he described his vision: it would be intimate, just him and me. It would be romantic, not fancy. He could see himself standing on the beach, wearing linen. I didn't care if we were wearing shorts and t-shirts—I was just happy that we were finally making it legal. But I did find it sweet that he was so excited that he had already planned the whole day out in his head.

The next morning I dragged him on our weekly walk to the beach. He hated to walk, but he always came because he knew how much it meant to me. Suddenly he stopped and, with a serious look on his face, said, "I know we never had a chance to have children, and I'm sorry. We would have made beautiful children. I know you stayed with me when I wasn't ready to trust, and I thank you. I couldn't imagine my life without you. If you would still like to have children, I was thinking we could adopt."

I was surprised and said, "Are you sure?"

"Yes," he said. "If you don't mind, can we adopt a boy?"

Daughter or son, I would love our child wholeheartedly. "Yes," I said, "I would love to adopt a boy with you."

When I was young, I thought that I wanted to have a daughter in the future, but after realizing how important it was to Bruce to have a boy, and having been unable to give him a child, I changed my mind. I knew adopting wouldn't be the same as raising a child that had been created by the two of us, but I was adopted and knew how much my parents loved me. I wanted to give the same to a little boy. He would know that someone wanted him, and he would grow up loved. We agreed that once we were settled in Hawaii and married, we would start the adoption process.

I had never seen Bruce more excited in all the time I had known him; he was looking forward to leaving LA and growing old in Hawaii. He had so many plans for when we moved to Hawaii, like taking dance lessons. I told him, "As long as it's dirty dancing."

He laughed and said, "Of course."

For the first time in all the years we had been together, we believed it was finally our time to live in peace. God knows we both deserved it. It would have been easy to give up long before, when times were tough. But from the day we met, we knew that what we had was worth fighting for, and we had proven it to each other many times over.

I was excited, but even while I was busy over the next two months packing up the house and getting my business ready to launch in Hawaii, I couldn't shake a feeling of dread that something bad was going to happen to me. I felt as if I were going to die. It was a feeling I'd never had before, and I couldn't explain it. One night, lying in bed with Bruce, I said, "If something happened to me, who would take care of you?"

"Nothing is going to happen to you," he assured me. "But if it did, know that I will be right there for you." I believed him. There had been times when I was seriously ill that he told me he would give his life to save me, and I knew he meant it. I relaxed and fell asleep, and dreamed of the life we would have together in Hawaii.

CHAPTER
FOURTEEN

In just two weeks we would be moving to Hawaii, and the house was completely packed. Bruce gave me a kiss and headed out to meet a friend for breakfast.

When he came home a few hours later, I noticed immediately that something wasn't right. He seemed confused. When I asked what was wrong, he replied, "I'm so tired; I'm going to go lie down." He headed to the bedroom, his gait slow and uncertain.

Maybe he had low blood sugar, I thought. I went to the kitchen and grabbed some juice and took it in to him. He drank it down, but as the minutes passed, there was no change. What if he'd had a stroke? I knew about some simple tests you could do: I asked him to smile, and then to close his eyes and raise both arms. His smile wasn't at all lopsided, and he was able to lift both his arms. It probably wasn't a stroke then.

"I'm so tired," he said again. "I just want to take a nap."

I left the room to let him rest, going in a couple of times to check and make sure he was okay. About twenty minutes after he lay down, I was standing on the deck when he emerged from the house and said, "I'm going to the guest house to cancel my yoga appointment today." Bruce had an office in the guest house in our backyard. As he made his way there slowly, something about the way he was walking and acting didn't make sense to me. I kept my eye on him and followed him into the backyard to make sure he was okay—and as I looked across the yard into the open door of the guest house, I watched him slump to the floor and begin to have convulsions.

I immediately called 911. When the paramedics arrived a few minutes later, I explained what I saw. "I've had seizures before," I said, "and this was a grand mal seizure." As I said the words, I wondered: how could such a healthy man, with no history of seizures, have such a bad grand mal? It was as I walked beside his stretcher on the way to the ambulance that my mind started going to the worst place. I fought the thoughts that arose. It wasn't a brain tumor, I told myself. Yes, I'd had a brain tumor growing up, and yes, at times it had caused grand mal seizures. But this couldn't be a brain tumor. I had been through a lifetime of medical problems and could handle anything that was thrown at me, but this was different. This was someone I loved more than life itself. He had to be okay.

Following the ambulance in my car, on the way to the hospital, I called my neurologist and told him that Bruce had a grand mal and something was very wrong. I told him that I felt it was something bad and was worried it might be a tumor. In the ER, Bruce was treated for seizures and had a CT scan. He had only a hazy memory of the seizure. "I wasn't feeling well when I got in the car to drive home," he recalled. "The last thing I remember is parking in front of the house and walking in the door."

"I'm so thankful you didn't have the grand mal before you got home. God knows what would have happened to you or someone else on the road," I said. When I was seventeen years old, I'd had a scary experience with a seizure: I was driving on the beltway at around 70 miles per hour, and the next thing I remembered, I was sitting in a parking lot, perfectly parked.

They came back with Bruce's CT scan, and it didn't show anything. They didn't know what caused the seizure. By then, Bruce was feeling better, only fatigued, so they sent him home and suggested he follow up with his regular doctor.

The entire ride home, my gut kept telling me that they had missed something, that there was more. As soon as I got home, I called my neurologist and had him schedule an MRI for Bruce right away.

The MRI revealed that there was, indeed, a brain tumor. The doctors couldn't confirm what type of tumor it was until it had been removed surgically and a biopsy had been performed. Bruce tried to act as though he was fine. Yet I knew him well enough to sense that he was scared and confused, though he didn't want me to see that. My mind immediately went to the worst place possible again: I remembered my uncle Glenn. When

I was nineteen, he had been diagnosed with a very aggressive brain cancer, Glioblastoma Multiforme, and lived only ten months. Bruce was sixty, and this type of tumor usually struck people between the ages of forty-five and seventy. Having seen the devastating effects it had on my uncle, I prayed to God this wasn't the type of tumor Bruce had.

From my time being treated at UCLA, I recalled the former dean of the medical school, Dr. Levey. I had always known Dr. Levey to be a kind man who strode the hallways talking to patients; he was truly the heart of UCLA. I called him at home and said, "I have been a patient at UCLA for more than twenty years. You guys have been my family, and I need you to please save my husband and get him the best for me." Within hours, Dr. Levey had assembled the finest team available.

Within five days, Bruce was at UCLA medical center being prepped for surgery. As they wheeled him away, I stopped to give him a hug and kiss and whispered to him, "You have been there for me all of these years—now it's my turn." He just smiled. I could tell from the look in his eye that he knew I was serious and that I would be there to care for him, come what may.

Bruce was in surgery for what seemed like forever. As the neurosurgeon, Dr. Yang, appeared at the door of the consultation room, I stood up to greet him. As he walked toward me, I knew it was bad. I sat down, and he gave me the worst news I could ever be given: "We received the biopsy results. I'm sorry, Bruce has Glioblastoma Multiforme." My heart dropped. I just couldn't believe this was happening to him. To us. This cancer had always been known as a death sentence.

In that instant, I knew that everything I had ever gone through was in order to prepare me for this. I had always questioned my purpose in life, and now I had the answer. The rest of our time together, I would dedicate my life to caring for Bruce. Everything I had ever endured in my life was to give me the strength to do this, to be there for him until the end.

Glioblastoma Multiforme, or GBM, is the cancer that took the lives of Senator Ted Kennedy and the son of Vice President Joe Biden, the former Delaware Attorney General Beau Biden. Striking two or three adults out of every 100,000 each year, GBM is known for being highly aggressive. Though it rarely travels to other parts of the body, it spreads rapidly through the supportive tissue of the brain. As the tumor grows, pressure builds inside the brain, and this can cause drowsiness and seizures, as it had for Bruce. It can also bring on headaches, nausea, vomiting, and double or blurred vision. Eventually, it can lead to changes in personality and mood, and difficulty with thinking, memory, and speech. Without exception, it is fatal. Even with surgery, chemotherapy, and radiation, most people can expect to live for only 15 months after being diagnosed.

The man I planned to spend the rest of my life with was going to die. We were only two weeks away from moving to Hawaii and adopting a son together. How could this be happening?

It felt like a cruel joke, one that I just couldn't understand. Our life together kept flashing through my mind. I couldn't imagine spending the rest of my days without Bruce.

The night of Bruce's diagnosis, I realized that the dread I had been feeling for two months, when I felt that I was going to die, was actually me feeling his death coming. We would always jokingly say that we were part of each other's DNA. I believed that in a completely different way now.

Bruce would have to wait for his surgical wounds to heal before he could begin chemotherapy and radiation. On the ride home, I put the top down so he could get some fresh air after being in the hospital. It was surreal; everything seemed to move in slow motion. Life had changed. As I looked over at him, it just didn't seem real that he had brain cancer. If someone had told me I had brain cancer, it wouldn't have been a surprise—but him?

My mind struggled to make sense of it all. I remembered how, a couple of months before he was diagnosed, we were in the garage working out what needed to be packed for the move to Hawaii and what we could leave in storage in Los Angeles. In the middle of a sentence, Bruce stopped and forgot what he was saying. A few minutes later, he went on with the conversation and was fine.

We have all lost our train of thought while we're speaking, but this time something about it caught my attention, and I'd kept my eye on him throughout the day to make sure he was okay. There had been many times in my life when I'd experienced an aura before a seizure, but at the time I would never have guessed that's what he was having. After his diagnosis, it made sense.

So did something else that I'd puzzled about for years. Whenever Bruce touched something cold, he didn't sense it as cold; he sensed it as pain. I told his surgeon that I thought Bruce might have had a lesion in his brain his whole life. "It's definitely a possibility," he'd replied.

I knew Bruce's prognosis was grim and that there were few treatment options and no cure. Despite all of the medical developments in recent decades that have given hope to people with some other types of cancer, little has changed for GBM patients. A chemotherapeutic drug called Temozolomide plus radiation increases survival by approximately two months, but beyond that there have been essentially no breakthroughs in either understanding or treating GBM for decades. Doctors told me that the drugs available to treat Bruce would only work for a period of time, and then they would start to fail and his cancer would return. They could switch drugs, but eventually there would be no more options left.

Part of the reason GBM is so hard to treat is that it's usually made up of a mixture of different types of malignant cells. While some of the cells may respond to one drug, other cells will continue to multiply quickly. There are clinical trials looking at new types of therapy targeting genes and the immune system, or using a special, highly focused type of radiation, or combining chemotherapy with vaccines. But even the advances that have been made in recent years have given most patients only a few extra months of life.

Nevertheless, I couldn't accept that there was so little treatment available to buy Bruce time. It was just too hard for me to wrap my head around the fact that we live in a technologically advanced world and that some of the most brilliant minds in cancer research are working on GBM, yet there still isn't a cure or even drugs that significantly extend survival. I was going to do everything I could. He was not going to die without a fight, and I was going to be right by his side, fighting for him.

I would spend night after night reading about everything that was being done in GBM research across the world. I would find that a promising trial was being planned—only to then learn that it was months, if not years, away. How bittersweet it would be if one of these trials resulted in a cure, and Bruce just missed out. A doctor had told me years before, "Unfortunately, in medicine someone has to die in order for there to be someone to live." Even though I knew what the doctor said was true, it just didn't seem fair that my husband would be the one losing his life.

I woke up one morning and knew that for Bruce's sake, I had to switch gears. I had to focus my energy on making sure he got the best possible care while he was alive. From that day on, I chose not to think about his prognosis. Instead, I decided to make the most of every moment that I was given with him. I started each day by waking him to give him his seizure medication, and I would say, "It's a beautiful day—let's go live it." And that's what we did. My new company was scheduled to launch in three months, but I canceled those plans and committed myself to taking care of Bruce like no other human on earth had ever been.

One night, we were lying in bed watching TV, and Bruce turned to me and said, "Remember the dream I told you I had when I was a kid?"

"The one where you were going to die, and I was there?" I said.

He nodded. "Well, it's now!" he said.

I held him and said, "I am so sorry you have to go through this. It isn't fair. But I can promise you, you will never have a want or need for as long as you live."

"I knew that I made the right choice to be with you when we met," he replied. "If anyone would be there when I needed them, I knew it would be you."

I was aware of what lay ahead, because I had seen what cancer had done to my uncle Glenn and also to my aunt Tomiko—the one who I had spent my childhood summers with. In 1990, she had been diagnosed with lung cancer. The surgeon had removed one of her lungs, and she had survived. But the fear of the cancer changed her forever. This once-vibrant woman now wanted only to stay at home. Even though she lived for seventeen years before succumbing to pneumonia, she had given up on living as soon as she was diagnosed. Cancer is such a merciless disease, destroying everything and anyone in its path. It slowly takes away a person's essence, and what remains is only a fragment of what the person once was. And when they have passed, it leaves those who are left behind to pick up the pieces and figure out how to go on without them.

When Bruce was feeling better after his surgery, he decided to go on a camping trip with some of his friends. I was concerned for his safety, but I also wanted him to have fun. He needed a break after what he had just gone through. The moment he drove off with his friends, I burst into tears. I felt as if he had just died. Then the worry set in: what if something happened to him and I wasn't there to take care of him?

I was relieved when he returned home. Not only had he been fine, he'd had a great time—and I also saw a change in him. It was as if getting away for a few days had given him the chance to start coming to terms with his diagnosis.

"Sweetie, it's time I get rid of my car," he announced. With seizures, he would never be able to drive again. We decided to donate it to a local church. Bruce acted like it wasn't a big deal, but I knew that, when he actually parted with his Suburban, it would be harder than he was portraying.

The day came when one of Bruce's friends, Tom, arrived to pick up the Suburban and drive it to the church.

"Tom's here for the car, if you want to say hi," I said as I walked into the room—and found Bruce in tears. He had realized that he was losing his independence, and his life had changed irrevocably.

I walked out to greet Tom. As I handed him the keys, I was then myself hit with deep emotion, standing in exactly the same spot on the driveway where Bruce had told me he loved me for the first time, almost twenty years before. He had had the Suburban for only two weeks when we first met. There were a lot of memories in that car for me—all the places that we had gone, all the weekend trips we had taken to get away from Los Angeles. Bruce loved to drive, so I'd never had to drive when he was with me. Now it would all be down to me.

As it started settling in for Bruce that he had the worst cancer on earth, he began to look at his life in a way he never had before. He would tell me that some of the people who had been friends for many years had changed. I thought maybe they hadn't changed but perhaps he had. Where before he had always tended to see only the best in everyone and had sometimes put up with behavior he probably shouldn't have, now he was seeing people more clearly.

He returned from playing golf with a longtime friend one day, and I asked, "Did you have fun?"

"I can't be around him anymore. He is so negative, I leave feeling stressed," he said. "He's always been this way. I guess I just don't have the tools to deal with it anymore." Bruce never called this friend again, and he stopped returning calls from several other friends. When I asked him why, he said, "I don't want to waste the time I have left on people who don't bring me peace."

I learned from Bruce's experiences that when you are given a terminal diagnosis, it changes you in ways that you can't explain. His priorities began to shift. Once, he had been very social. Now, he told me, "I don't want to be with anyone but you."

"But Bruce, is that really fair?" I said. "People want to have time with you."

When people came to visit, I didn't turn them away, because I didn't want to hurt their feelings. But I was the one in the middle, trying to keep the peace. When his guests left, Bruce would angrily tell me he didn't want them to come back and that he did not want them in his life any longer.

On the one hand, it was sad to see Bruce angry and disappointed with some of the people who had been a big part of his life for years. On the other, I felt that he was finally seeing the truth about some of the people he'd kept around him, and some of these people had caused tension in my own life. Out of the blue one night when we were lying in bed, he said, "You have a big heart—make sure you live your life with only good people surrounding you." I knew he was making a reference to someone who had been part of his life for years who had made things difficult for me. He acknowledged how much this person had affected me and said he hoped that I would move on and not let this person impact my life in the future. "You deserve better," he said.

CHAPTER FIFTEEN

Within weeks, Bruce had fully recovered from the surgery and was getting back to his old self. Most people said they had no idea that he'd even had surgery. There was a saying that he used all the time, especially when he thought a situation might be more complicated than it appeared on the surface: "We don't know the full story." When I looked at Bruce, who was in the best shape of his life, that sentence played over and over in my head.

I wanted him to carry on with normal life for as long as he was physically capable. Deep down, he knew his life was never going to return to normal, but I think he'd made a decision that he wasn't going to stress over it. I scheduled his chemotherapy and radiation appointments. "Let's kick cancer's butt," he said.

The night before each treatment, while he slept, I would prepare our meals for the following day. The morning of the treatment, I would wake and pack everything up, get him ready, and off to the hospital we would go. I would usually make enough food for the doctors and nurses, too. I wanted to give back for all their hard work and effort and let them know that I cared about them, too.

There will always be a special place in my heart for doctors and nurses. They wake up every day and go to work to care for people who need them, and some days they are able to make their patient's day a better one. Because I had been a patient at UCLA for more than twenty years, when I walked through the hospital, it was rare not to pass someone I knew. Whether from radiology, anesthesiology, or doctors' offices, they always treated me as if I were family. Some gave me hugs. They would ask how Bruce was doing and tell me they were praying for him. Their support meant a lot to me and to Bruce.

Every doctor's visit, Bruce was examined and asked a litany of neurological questions, the same ones I had been asked for so many years. For me, it was like looking back in time. There was a strange familiarity to the ritual, and it brought me comfort.

"Spell 'world.'"

"Spell 'world' backward."

"What day is it?"

"Can you touch your finger to your nose?"

Some days while he lay in bed during his treatment, I would find myself staring at him as he slept, proud of him for his inner strength. No matter what he was going through during his cancer, he never once complained. I didn't know if I could be the same.

We would spend most of the day at the hospital, and when we got home, we would be exhausted. I would be glad that I had made dinner the night before. I was very serious about the foods Bruce ate, making sure he stayed healthy. In the time he battled cancer, he was never sick one day from the chemotherapy. After dinner, we would lie in bed and watch TV together. It was very simple, and I didn't want it any other way.

During breakfast one morning, we talked about how he was feeling about it all. "I don't have control over this. I can only live the life I'm given, and God must have a plan," said Bruce. Before he was diagnosed, he had a weekly schedule of tennis, yoga, and sessions with a private trainer. He had the body of a forty-year-old. "Perhaps I knew something was about to happen and I needed to be in the best shape of my life to get through it," he said.

Bruce didn't think he was going to die. He thought he was going to be the one that beat this horrid disease, and I certainly wasn't going to tell him different. All he had left was hope, and I didn't want to take that away from him. I was going to be there, supporting him every step of the way, until he said, "It's time."

He would have monthly MRIs to check the progression of his cancer, and I believed that when his tumor stopped responding to the treatment and began to grow, the stress of knowing that would prevent him from being able to live the life he had left. So I spoke privately with his neuro-oncologist. "When the time comes, I don't want him to know," I said. "No matter what his MRIs show, I want to tell him that the tumor's holding, and to keep fighting." I knew I would feel terrible for not telling him the truth, but I wanted him to savor every moment of life he had left. I didn't want to take away what little hope he may have had. I made a resolution that I would put on a smile and continue fighting with him.

One week into Bruce's treatment, as usual I had woken early to get ready. As I had lowered myself into the bathtub, I'd slipped and fallen, taking all of my weight on my right elbow. I had seen my shoulder jerk upward, all the way to my ear, and known right away that I was in trouble. I had been in a lot of pain, but I didn't have time to stop and do anything about it, because I had to get Bruce to the hospital. I had held my arm close to my body and taken him for his treatment. I continued to do this for the next month, until he finished his course of radiation. I had wanted to make sure he had an advocate with him at all times, so there was no chance that anything could go wrong.

Once Bruce had finished his radiation treatments, I was able to schedule an appointment with an orthopedic surgeon at UCLA. I had an MRI, which showed that I had torn my rotator cuff and labrum, which hold the shoulder in place. I was booked in to have surgery a few days later.

"You need to prepare for this," the surgeon told me.

"I'll be fine. I've had brain surgery, and if I can go through that torture, shoulder surgery will be nothing," I replied.

"No, you *really* have to prepare," he said.

The day of my surgery, Bruce insisted on going with me to the hospital. He wasn't allowed to drive, so we took a cab. I remember that morning so clearly; he told me he loved me at least three times on the way to the hospital. I knew he was scared that something might happen to me while under anesthesia. For years, when I would be wheeled into surgery, Bruce would express his concerns and tell me his life wouldn't be the same if something happened to me. I would joke and say, "They have been trying to get rid of me for years, and they haven't been successful yet. I'll see you soon." It always seemed to make him feel better.

I have never had fear going into surgery. For me, it was all about choosing the best surgeons I could and having faith they would do a good job. Except this time, it wasn't about me. If something did happen, who would take care of Bruce? Who could ever care for and love him the way I did?

"I'm not going anywhere," I assured him. But just in case, I said a few prayers to God to please watch over him while I was in surgery. Before they put me under, I said one last prayer asking God to please protect me so I could be there for Bruce.

When I woke in recovery and was trying to focus and come out of the fog of anesthesia, Bruce's face was the first thing I saw, and I felt him holding my hand. As things started becoming clearer, I realized I wasn't feeling any pain. What was the surgeon talking about? This was nothing.

Later that night, when we were back at home, I started feeling pain of an intensity I had never in my life felt before. With every movement I made, the pain went deep into my heart. I have a bad reaction to opioid painkillers like the ones they sent me home with, but Tylenol and ice weren't helping. I called the surgeon and told him I was in an unbearable amount of pain, and he suggested that I try taking the opioid pain medication. I was desperate at that point, so I took a half a pill. Ten minutes later, when I was standing in the bathroom with Bruce as he brushed his teeth, I began to feel light-headed.

"Are you okay?" he asked.

I started to drop to the floor, but he grabbed me in time and sat me on the toilet. When I could walk, he helped me get comfortable on the sofa that was to be my bed for the next couple of weeks.

When I went to my post-op appointment with the surgeon, he asked, "How are you feeling?"

All I could say was, "Have mercy." I was in tears from the pain. For a moment, I thought he was going to tell me "I told you so." But he didn't. He had sympathy for the pain I was in. After examining my shoulder, he got a concerned look on his face. My shoulder had frozen.

"Melissa, you're going to require another surgery in six months," he said. I couldn't possibly conceive of going through that pain again. But I also knew that I couldn't live with a shoulder that didn't function.

I never considered taking care of Bruce work, because I enjoyed it. There was nothing that was going to stop me from looking after him, though there were times after my shoulder surgery that I thought I was going to mentally break from the pain. But all I would have to do is look at him, and I would remember that he needed me to care for and love him, and that this was so much harder for him. I knew that I would eventually heal and be fine, but he wouldn't.

From the time Bruce was diagnosed, every week my friend Boris, who was an oncologist at another well-known hospital, would check in to see how Bruce was doing. He knew Bruce had the best doctor out there for his cancer and was confident he was in good hands. I believe he was mostly checking in on me to see how I was doing. Knowing that I was caring for Bruce by myself, he was concerned that I was going to burn out, and he was probably right. One afternoon as Bruce slept, I went to the beach to pick up lunch. I wasn't allowed to drive, so I walked, even though I was still in a lot of pain. When I returned an hour later, I realized that walking was exactly what I needed; it helped me to work off all of the stress that I was feeling about Bruce's illness.

Six months after my shoulder surgery, I had the second operation. The pain was bad but nowhere near as bad as the first time. Yet one week later, I could tell it hadn't been successful. Once again, my shoulder had frozen. I decided that I would deal with it another time and continue focusing on Bruce. I was still in pain, couldn't lie on my right side, and wasn't able to turn my arm. But I could lift my arm above my head, and that was enough to take care of Bruce. I would figure the rest out later.

Soon after my second surgery, we were at home late one afternoon, and I heard a noise. As I turned to look at Bruce, I saw that he was on the floor having a grand mal seizure. I cleared a space around him so that he couldn't hurt himself and called 911.

At UCLA, they admitted Bruce for observation. I was still in pain from the surgery and was in a sling, but nothing was going to keep me from being by his side. He had always been there for me during the darkest times of my life, encouraging me to believe that things would get better, so there was no doubt I was going to do the same for him. It didn't matter what I was going through; all that mattered was making sure he didn't feel alone or scared. That night, I slept on a sofa in his room. The nurses could see I was in pain and did their best to make me comfortable.

Two days later, Bruce was feeling better and showing no signs of having another seizure, so he was released. That night, I could tell he was happy to be home in his own bed. As we lay there, I looked at him, thinking: Is this really happening? How could he have such a deadly cancer? He turned to me and said with such conviction, "God almighty, I love you." I fell apart inside, knowing I was going to lose him and there was nothing I could do to stop this godforsaken cancer. I wanted to scream out at that moment and ask, "Why?" But I had to hold it together for him. Every day I put on a smile, but inside it was killing me to know he was going to die.

☆   ☆   ☆

Years before, I had asked Bruce, "If you were given thirty days to live, how would you live them and with whom would you spend those days?" He had said, "In Hawaii, lying on the beach with you." During his treatment, when we needed an escape from the hospital, we took a trip to our house in Hawaii. When we arrived, Bruce would do what he always did: reach up and pick a flower from the plumeria tree, put it in my hair, give me a kiss, and say, "Welcome home."

I have always been an early riser, and Bruce was a night owl; he liked the quiet of the night, and I like the peace of the morning. In Hawaii, I would wake, sit on the beach, and take photos of the sunrise. Bruce would wake around 10:00 AM, and I would climb into bed and show him the photos I had taken. It was my way of experiencing the sunrise with him. Being a photographer, he would smile and say it was sweet that I would do this for him. Or sometimes, he would say, "When I was younger, this is what I would see as I was just getting home from my night out." In the evening, I would play music, and we would dance around the living room like kids. When he got tired, he would sit on the sofa and listen to me sing. He was such a trooper—he did it for me because he knew it brought me joy.

Our house was on the windward side of the beach, so there was usually a breeze, but during one trip to Hawaii, we had Kona winds. This is when the wind direction gets reversed, and on our side of the island, the air is stagnant. I remember one particular night: it was hot and humid; as he held me, I felt his body sweating next to mine; and, for a moment, I allowed myself to forget the reality. I pictured in my mind when we first met and the closeness we felt with each other—a closeness when two became one, and there was a fulfillment of love that was beyond words. I wanted it to never end, but I had to accept reality; I wondered how much time we had left with each other. After Bruce's diagnosis, everything became more important. The hardest days we went through had brought us a love that was worth every battle we had faced. We wouldn't have traded a moment of it for anything in the world.

We returned to Los Angeles in time for Bruce to go to chemotherapy the next morning. Just as we were getting back into the groove of the faster pace, we discovered that our house had termites and required tenting. I made arrangements for us to stay at a hotel close to a busy shopping area near our home in Santa Monica, so we could walk to everything and Bruce could get some exercise. It was for only two days, but it was like a mini-vacation. We didn't know at the time that it would be the last one we would ever have together.

Bruce's chemotherapy drug was no longer working, so he started a clinical trial. Within a week, I could see the drug was starting to cause side effects, such as his platelet level dropping very low, so his doctor switched him to another drug. It meant taking him to chemotherapy treatments every two weeks instead of once a month. I didn't care. I would have gone once a day if it would buy him time.

I knew that eventually, as Bruce's tumor grew, he would become unable to speak. One morning as we drove to UCLA, I asked him, "If something were to happen to you, what sign would you give me to let me know you were still here with me?"

"I can't tell you, but I promise you will know it's me."

During dinner one night, I noticed that Bruce was quiet. A few minutes later, he reached over to hold my hand. "I'm sorry we never got to move to Hawaii and marry," he said. "I don't want to die without you knowing how much I love you. Will you marry me?" Of course, I said "Yes!"

After seventeen years together, we already felt as though we were married, but we were excited on our wedding day. Bruce had always introduced me as his wife, but now I was going to legally be his wife, and he would be my husband for the time he was given on this earth. We cried throughout the entire ceremony, and there were a few tears shed by our friend Brian, who was our witness, and by the woman who performed the ceremony in our dining room.

It was Bruce's wish that it be just the two of us, as he had planned when we were to marry in Hawaii. At first, I didn't understand why he didn't want friends and family there, but after the ceremony, I could see why. When I was young, I'd dreamed of one day having a big wedding—but that would have been nothing compared to the intimacy we had that day. I couldn't have imagined a more perfect wedding. In some ways, we were glad that we hadn't married all those years before, because it could never have been as special as that day. As the woman who performed the ceremony was leaving, she turned around with tears in her eyes and said, "This day changed my life." Well, it changed mine, too.

The next morning, when I woke and turned to him, I was surprised to see that he'd woken before me. He smiled and said, "Good morning, Mrs. Ayres. I wish I had married you when we met, and I'm sorry." I understood why he hadn't been able to trust back then, and it didn't matter. In reality, it was just paper. His trust and dedication now proved to me how much he loved me.

CHAPTER SIXTEEN

Bruce was starting to have trouble keeping his balance, and I could tell it was time for him to start using a wheelchair. "I don't need it," he would say. It was a struggle for him to accept it, because it meant he was losing more of his independence, and that scared him.

Once he realized that the only way I could continue to care for him was if he used a wheelchair, he no longer had a problem with using it. I lifted him into the chair three times a day and wheeled him onto the deck so we could do his physical therapy. He wanted to stay strong, and I was going to help the best I could. In the chair on the deck, I would have him do leg lifts and arm raises, and when I put him in bed, I would stretch his muscles out. Most days, I turned the deck into a full-service spa. I shaved his face out there, trimmed his hair, and gave him facials and body scrubs.

Sometimes we would just sit out there and listen to the birds. One day, I could hear this little chirping sound that didn't sound like a bird, and I couldn't figure out where it was coming from.

"They are hummingbirds," Bruce told me.

"Hummingbirds don't make a sound, do they?" I said. I didn't believe him, but a few minutes later, I was amazed when a tiny hummingbird landed on a branch close to me, and I could hear the chirping sound. Bruce was right!

These moments that we spent out on the deck enjoying the simple things in life were precious to both of us. I now had an even deeper understanding of the care and devotion that my cousin Voight had shown for my uncle Glenn in his final months with GBM decades before. One of Glenn's passions was fishing, and when the days were sunny and warm, Voight would take him down to the lake so they could fish. When Uncle Glenn became too ill to walk, my cousin would pick him up and carry him down to the water. One day while they were sitting by the lake, my uncle said, "You don't have to do this for me."

"Yes I do," replied Voight. "When I was a little boy, you used to carry me down to the water so I could fish, so I want to do the same for you."

With the wheelchair, it was a little bit harder getting Bruce to UCLA for chemotherapy, but I figured out pretty quickly how to do it by myself. I started waking up an hour earlier to feed and bathe Bruce in bed, and dress him. Then I would wedge the chair's wheels between the bedroom wall and the bed, stand on the bed above him, pull him close to me, and while holding him up, I would step off the bed and turn him around to face me. I would then reach under his arms, and with my feet planted on the floor, lift him into the wheelchair. It was hard to believe that a 5'7" and 125-pound girl could lift a man who was 6'1" and 180 pounds, but strangely, with the right leverage, I could do it with ease.

I would wheel him down a ramp to the car, put the car's top down, lift him into the car, put the chair in the garage, put the top up on the car, and drive to UCLA. When we got to the hospital, I would find a wheelchair, bring it back to the car, put the top down, lift him into the chair, and put the top up again. After his MRI or chemotherapy, the whole process would be repeated several times again, until I got him into bed at home. I'm not sure how many times I lifted him in a day, but it never once felt like work. There are no words that could ever describe how grateful I was to be able to hold him close to me and care for him.

During one of Bruce's MRIs, I scheduled a medical test for myself at UCLA. Months earlier, I had complained to my doctor that there was blood in my urine, but he didn't feel it was anything to worry about. Because it had continued, I became concerned, and now I was to have a cystoscopy, a test in which a scope is guided up the urethra to take images inside the bladder. As the doctor guided the scope, he saw that there was a growth there, stopped the procedure, and referred me to the Urology department, where they scheduled me for surgery.

I was not one to worry about anything medical until someone gave me good reason to; after all the years of medical procedures I had gone through, I had learned not to borrow trouble. Still, the night before the surgery, I was very stressed. My concern wasn't for me; it was for Bruce. What if this turned out to be cancer? Who would be there to take care of him? I prayed that night for God to spare me once again, just so I could care for Bruce. I asked that if He had to take me, to please let it be after Bruce was no longer here.

I had to be at the hospital early that morning, and Bruce came with me. Once again, I awoke after the surgery to see Bruce's face. It felt like forever until I received the biopsy results, and when it did, it seemed my prayers had been answered. I would just need to return in a few months for a follow-up to make sure there was no new growth.

I was finding it increasingly difficult to convince myself that all the time I had spent having tests and treatment at UCLA somehow made it easier being there now with Bruce. In reality, it was incredibly hard. When I was going through medical procedures, I could handle the hospital. This was different because it was the man I loved fighting for every extra day of life he could get. There were times when I was beyond exhausted, but I was determined that he would know he was cared for and loved by me until the end. I couldn't imagine it being any other way, and I know he couldn't, either.

I had always been very private when I was going through medical problems myself, but when I was alone at home caring for Bruce, I realized that I needed to reach out for the support of others. I decided to share Bruce's and my journey on Facebook, and it all started with this one post:

> Anyone who knows me would know how private I am. It is awful to watch someone I love slowly die and there is nothing I can do to save him. I pray that no one ever has to watch the one they love die.

I was comforted by the comments I received. Actually, I don't know how I would have been able to get through that time without everyone's support around me. I would read my friends' comments late at night when Bruce slept, and they gave me strength on the hardest days:

> Some live their entire life without "being" in love. They may feel it, they may have it, but some never "become" in a love transformed. Your very being transmits the energy of your love . . . to him . . . to us . . . everywhere . . . and nothing can destroy it. Thank you for your example. We are humbled to share what little comfort and support we can.

> It's a membership to a club nobody wants to join. Not everyone is able to deal with being a caregiver

when a loved one is dying, especially caring 24/7. Nothing prepares you, nothing. It's the best of times and the worst all rolled into one. It is good days and bad, crying and laughter all within seconds, a roller coaster of emotions. It's okay to be happy and sad and even angry. You are handling this with such grace.

As soon as he leaves you in this life, his love and compassion will always follow you. He will never leave your side. He will be the wind whispering in your ear. He will be the sunlight in your eyes of each waking day. He will walk beside you as he has always done and wait for you until eternity. For you are truly his soul and waits for you to finish this dance. Life continues beyond this horizon.

I wished there was a secret I could discover, a way to make time stand still so that Bruce could stay with me forever, or a way to rewind to the day he'd had his first seizure and rewrite his future. Yet I was also grateful to have been given quality time to spend with him. We had time to tell each other everything we wanted. I found more and more that he was telling me things he wanted to get off his chest—how he really felt about people and about the mistakes he had made in his life. He told me, "We went through a lot of hard times together, but I don't regret a moment." He spoke of what we had endured in our relationship and the role that some of the people who were in his life had played in our struggles, and he apologized to me. I knew he was feeling a lot of guilt, but the past didn't matter. All that mattered was that he knew how much I loved him and that I would be there for him no matter what.

Moments later, he looked over at me with tears in his eyes and said, "I knew exactly who you were from the moment we met and that I was going to love you." I knew the same and was glad he was in my life. There was truly no place I would have rather been. Every morning I woke to see him smile, when so many going through this wouldn't be able to. He just wanted to live the life he had left with only love, and that is what I was going to give him.

We all have this idea when we are young of what true love is. We are led to believe it's a romantic dinner by candlelight and a dozen red roses. But now I know that true love isn't what we read or see in the movies. It's far deeper, and nothing like I had expected when I was younger. True love is when you have had a hard day, and your partner wants to do everything possible to make it better for you. It's when you've spent hours cooking and, without you asking, he washes the dishes to show you how much he appreciates all you do. It's lying on a blanket on the beach looking up at the stars, not having to say a word, knowing you couldn't imagine being anywhere else. It's when another person's happiness means more than your own. It's wanting to do everything possible on this earth for someone, so he knows he could never feel more loved. Love can suspend time, making the whole world stand still. It can be just a kind word or a soft kiss on your neck, but there is one thing for certain: when you find the one that touches your heart, you will never be the same again.

☆   ☆   ☆

It had been almost two years since Bruce had been diagnosed, and every morning during that time I had woken with a purpose. I would start by making him breakfast and preparing his medication, and then I'd go into the bedroom. He would give me a big hug and kiss and say, "I love you," and it would always make my day. We spent every waking moment together, and there was nothing we hadn't said to each other that needed to be said.

Even when all he had left was the function of his left arm, I looked forward to waking him. I would give him a hug and kiss, and he would pull his arm out from under the covers, put it around me, and give me a kiss on the forehead. We did that every day until he wasn't able to anymore. My heart broke each time I walked into the room and knew that I was never going to receive a hug or kiss from him again. They would now be only a memory from that day forward.

I bathed, fed, and took care of him, and if possible I would have done it forever. I was happy to know that he had chosen me to care for him in the time he'd been given, and I saw that my life had been forever changed by it.

One day, I was in the kitchen preparing Bruce's lunch, and I heard him calling my name. I walked into the bedroom and asked, "Do you need something?"

"No, I just wanted you to know how much I love you and thank you for caring for me." My heart just melted. He was the only man who could render me speechless with his love. "I know that if you hadn't been in my life, everyone else would have brought in home care to take care of me," he said. "And I would have given up."

I was sad he felt that way. I could only imagine how vulnerable he felt now that he was no longer able to walk or do anything for himself and was completely dependent on someone else to care for him. "I'm not going anywhere. I'll always be here to care for you," I assured him.

That night, we were watching a movie, and as I looked over at him, I saw that he was crying. I held him, and he said, "Am I going to die?"

"I don't know," I said, "but I promise I'll keep fighting for you to stay. I sure hope you don't go, because I will miss you terribly."

"I will miss you, too," he said.

On one of our visits to UCLA, Bruce's doctor had reviewed his latest MRI with me. I didn't need for him to tell me the results. I could see the tumor was growing. There were no more treatment options left, and Bruce wouldn't have much time. We decided to continue his chemotherapy until he was no longer able to go to the hospital, because I could see he still wanted to be here.

As I was getting ready to head back to the room to get Bruce ready to go home, Dr. Cloughesy pulled me aside and said, "You know that I have been doing this for a long time. I want you to know that I have never met anyone like you in my entire career. I have never seen a patient more loved and cared for in my life." I was pretty sure that was the kindest thing anyone had ever said to me. On the hardest days, I would think about what Bruce's doctor said to me, and it would give me the strength I needed to continue caring for him.

Bruce was always the perfect patient. He never once complained or said, "Why me?" He did whatever I needed him to do, and he did it with such grace. I would tell him how proud I was of him, and he would say, "It's all you." But I knew it was him. He was being driven by a strong desire not to leave.

When I heard the news that Vice President Joe Biden's son Beau had been diagnosed with GBM, my heart broke for him and his family. Sadly, I already knew what they were going to experience. Just like every family who has a loved one diagnosed with GBM, the Bidens would be overwhelmed by the feeling of helplessness that comes from knowing there is no cure and that treatment can only buy time, just as in Bruce's case. Then frustration hit me. I thought: when even the most powerful people in the world are unable to save their loved ones, we really have a problem, and something needs to be done.

How much longer do we have to wait, and how many more people need to die?

Because GBM is relatively rare compared to other types of cancer, it has seldom grabbed headlines, except when Ted Kennedy passed away in 2009, and then Beau Biden in 2015. Very little money has been allocated to fighting it, and that has hampered the research and development of effective treatments. But hopefully all of that is about to change. I recently became involved with AGILE, a team of more than 130 neurosurgeons, neuro-oncologists, and other scientists who are working together as volunteers determined to go after this monster of a cancer and put an end to it once and for all.

AGILE is conducting a coordinated global adaptive clinical trial that will be faster and more efficient than previous trials at testing drugs and combinations of drugs on patients with GBM. This means that promising treatments will move more quickly to the next phase of testing, and ineffective treatments will be dropped more quickly. AGILE's trial also aims to identify GBM biomarkers that can be targeted using precision medicine. By offering treatments based on the individual make-up of a patient's tumor, precision medicine promises to revolutionize the treatment of cancer. Interestingly, success for GBM AGILE could also pave the way for understanding and treating other cancers, especially those that are considered rare.

After he was diagnosed, Bruce and I rarely spoke about death or cancer, focusing instead on living each day. But I wanted to know how he was feeling. "Are you afraid to die?" I asked him as we lay together.

"No, because I have lived an amazing life. But I'm afraid to leave, knowing you will be sad," he answered. "I need you to know, I am with you always. When I'm no longer here, all you have to do is dream, and I will be there."

With tears running down my face, I asked, "Do you feel loved?"

He stared at me and said, "So loved." That was all I ever needed to know.

I had set up a monitor so that no matter which room I was in, Bruce could communicate with me. One morning, I was in the kitchen preparing his breakfast and medication, and when I heard him on the monitor, I could tell he was starting to lose his ability to speak. His voice was soft and whispery as he tried to say my name. It was now "Issa, Issa." There were no words that could express the love I felt for him then. I waited my life for this love, and now I was watching it slowly slip away from me, and it just wasn't fair. I prayed that each day would pass slowly and that he would be given more time. But I wanted each moment he had left on earth to be the best he could have.

In many ways, the past two years had been a blur. I had never left his side for more than one hour a week to go to the market and run to the drug store for his weekly supplies, and I didn't even want to be apart from him for that hour. When I arrived home, I'd park in the garage, grab the groceries, and stand at the back door saying a prayer that he was okay. I would breathe a sigh of relief as I entered the bedroom to see he was quietly sleeping.

Some days, I wondered if I would be able to watch him die. But then I would lie next to him and sense how much he needed me, and I would realize that God had given me the strength I needed to face the darkest hour.

The holidays were approaching, and I knew they would be Bruce's last. Wanting to do something special for him, I decided to make a movie of his life. While running back and forth to care for him, I sat on the floor of the garage, going through thousands of photos from the day he was born. I selected hundreds of them, spent the next two days scanning them, and then made a movie out of them. I was exhausted at the end of each day, but what I was doing for him was worth it, and I would never get the chance to do it again. As I would climb into bed beside him, he would say to me in a whispery voice, "I love you." He would always say it twice. It was just like when he used to give me two greeting cards and say, "One wasn't enough."

The holidays came, and I played the movie for him. He had produced commercials and been very good at it, and I hoped that he would like what I'd created for him. He lay still and stared, not saying a word. When the movie ended, I looked at him and asked, "What do you think?"

He said, "Beautiful."

It was the last word he would ever speak.

Although we had already said everything we needed to say to each other, I wanted to make sure he never forgot how much I loved him. Knowing that he would be able to hear me until the end, I would lie beside him and tell him that if anything ever happened to him, I would be holding him when God took him. At night, I would sing, "You are my sunshine" softly in his ear—only I would leave off the ending—and it would make him smile.

Lying next to him, it was hard to accept that we were never going to have another conversation again. In my head, I knew that nothing stays the same and life is forever changing—but in my heart, I wasn't ready for it. I just wanted everything to be the way it used to be.

During our first year together, Bruce had said to me, "You can tell someone you love them too much," and I had replied, "Never." Now, as I sat on the edge of the bed feeding him, he would just stare at me. I knew it was his way of telling me that he was still there and he loved me. I would gently touch his face so he could feel me, and then I would tell him how much I loved him. Even though he already knew, I was going to tell him over and over, because when he was gone, I wouldn't be able to again. With every breath I took, I just wanted him to feel as though he was the most loved human on this earth.

There were so many things I would miss after he passed—the special things he did to let me know how much he loved me, the dedication he showed—but most of all, I would miss the warm hugs on a bad day and the power of his kiss, which was something I had never experienced with anyone before.

There was one thing I knew without a doubt: if I had the opportunity, I would have given the rest of my life to care for him. There was nothing I wouldn't have done; my life was complete when I was with him. Whether he was healthy or diagnosed with cancer, I loved him the same. I felt I had already lived many lifetimes and wasn't afraid to die.

So when I lay next to him, helplessly watching the days he had left on earth dwindling, I would pray to God to take years off my life so he could have more.

Bruce had always loved the feeling of clean, crisp cotton sheets, so I changed his linens every day. If he had to be stuck in bed, I wanted him to be as comfortable as possible. It was a lot of work to change them, but I had learned how to do it by watching the nurses as they did it for me when I was a patient in the hospital. I would make my side of the bed first, roll him onto his side, pull the old sheets out from under him, make his side of the bed, and then roll him back. Then I would lie next to him, which was my favorite part.

I lifted him in the bed and turned him frequently, but one day I realized he had the start of a small bed sore. I got all of Bruce's medical supplies from a home health care service, so I called them, and they delivered a supply of patches to place on the sore. As I turned him the next morning, I saw that the sore had grown five times in size. Bruce's skin was inflamed, and I was livid. I immediately called the service's triage nurse, who explained that they must have dropped off the wrong supplies. The patch had caused moisture to get trapped close to Bruce's skin, which had caused the large sore. I wanted to say, "You think?" but I tried to keep my cool and just get the situation handled. They sent out a wound-care nurse and the proper supplies. But the damage had already been done. It would require many applications of cream to protect him from getting an infection. Fortunately, I managed to keep his skin clean, and the wound stopped spreading.

Two weeks passed, and as I fed Bruce, I could see he was having a hard time swallowing. It was time to stop all solid foods and switch him to only liquids. He had no problem with that, because he loved protein shakes. That lasted for about a week. Then he was no longer able to take in fluids, and I knew that he didn't have much time left.

One morning when I went into the bedroom to clean his wound, I started to see a change happening, and I knew what was coming. His body was preparing to die. His wound was now turning black, and I could see his body was starting to shut down. It was hard to know how much time he had left, and I tried not to think about it. I wouldn't give myself time to cry now. My only focus was to make sure he didn't suffer or have pain.

I had been in the house alone with Bruce for quite a while, watching his time run out. These were some of the hardest days of my life. Late one day, as I turned him on his side to apply the cream to his wound, a large patch of his skin came off in my hands. I fell to the ground in tears, wondering if he was in any pain. I have always been the person everyone says they want to have around during a crisis, because I remain calm. This was different. I was watching the man I loved fall apart in front of me, and I was helpless to stop it and angry that the cancer was winning. I never like to lose, and I hated that I was powerless.

To make sure the area stayed clean, I placed gauze over the wound. Then I turned him on his back and lay down next to him. I held him and told him how sorry I was that he was going through this and that it wasn't fair. I could hear him in my mind telling me, "Life isn't always fair."

I hated when he would tell me that, and I would say to him, "I have always felt life should never know pain and sadness. Why do they have to exist in the first place?"

He would say, "I don't know that answer."

I lay as close as I could possibly get to Bruce, pressing my body against his. I didn't want him to forget the feeling of our bodies touching.

That night I watched as he peacefully slept and God prepared his body and soul. I reached over to hold his hand and felt a deep sadness as I remembered that he was no longer able to hold mine. I felt blessed, because Bruce's love forever changed my life, but at the same time, it was the worst feeling in the world, because he was dying and I couldn't save him. I lay next to him with my face pressed up against his, sinking into him, trying to take in as much as I could in the time we had left.

During Bruce's last week, I could see that he was dying but that he was holding on for me. It was Sunday when I began to tell him that it was okay for him to go with God and be in peace, as I was falling apart. But he knew I didn't really want him to go, and he kept fighting to stay. Every day for the next three days, I continued to tell him that it was okay. By Thursday evening, I had nothing left. I felt as though I was dying, too. I reached down into the deepest part of my soul and prayed for God to give me the strength I needed. I had never felt such emptiness.

I began pleading with Bruce, "I love you more than life itself, but you have to go, because it's killing me to watch you die. I will be with you one day, baby." Of course, I didn't want him to die; I wanted him to be with me forever, and if given the choice, I would have cared for him for the rest of time. But I knew there was no quality of life left for him, and he was going to a place that was kinder. Our souls were connected for life and always had been, and I knew we would find each other again one day. He had walked a lonely road before we met, and I was glad to have been the one who was waiting at the end of his journey.

That night, I spoke with his nurse at UCLA. "He doesn't have much time left," I told her.

"He does not want to leave this love," she replied.

We learn to have faith that after this life we go to a place that is beautiful and filled with peace. But there is always a part of us that wonders, *Is there?* Maybe Bruce was struggling with the risk of leaving what he had here in this world for the unknown. Maybe he was sad that he wasn't being given the choice to stay.

As the sun rose the next morning, I knew it was going to be his last day on this earth and he may have only hours left. I grabbed the music we had always listened to together, because I wanted his final hours to be filled with as much love that he could take in. It was going to be just him and me until the end, just as he said he wanted it to be. I put his arm around me and played him the song he played me the day after I moved in, "Stars Are Ours" by The Nylons. Then I stayed there and played all the songs we had listened to over the almost twenty years we were together.

It was a beautiful and horrible day all at the same time. I never left his side for a moment; I wanted to take in every possible second that was given to him, grasping as if I were fighting for my life, too. I took in every scent, and I thought about his voice and prayed that time wouldn't take my memories of him away.

I kissed him, so that I would never forget the feeling of his lips on mine. I hoped that on the journey he was about to take, he would not forget the love I felt for him. I tried to be brave for him, but inside I was breaking apart.

As I held him, I felt him go. The song that was playing was Enya's "May It Be." It was the song I had asked him to play if something ever happened to me. I believe that he chose to pass when that song began to play, as his way of saying, "I am going to be okay, and so are you."

I tried to tell myself that he was gone, but my heart just didn't want to believe it. I lay there in disbelief. It didn't matter that I had known throughout the day that Bruce was dying—it just couldn't possibly be real. I prayed over and over to God that he please take care of Bruce's soul and love him as much as I did. As I lay there holding him, a favorite quote of mine, by Judy Garland, came into my mind: "For it was not into my ear you whispered, but into my heart. It was not my lips you kissed but my soul."

I had never been more devastated and fulfilled in my entire life—devastated because the man who was part of my soul was gone and I would never be able to hold or touch him again, and fulfilled because I was blessed to have experienced a love so deep that it altered who I was forever.

Everything was moving in slow motion. I had prepared in advance to call the hospice to record the time of Bruce's death. I picked up the phone and dialed, even though I didn't want to.

The nurse asked, "When would you like for us to schedule him to be picked up?"

I thought: Picked up? How was it possible that he was gone, and they needed to take him away? It just didn't make sense. How could this be?

I needed time with Bruce to say goodbye, so I told her four hours. In the dimly lit room, I lay against his body, holding him, because I felt that I needed to keep him warm. Though he was gone, I was still trying to care for him. As I lay there, I could feel that his soul was no longer there, and all that was left was the shell that God had given him in order to stand on this earth. Yet I continued to hold him until they came, knowing I would never be able to again. I recalled his voice, the feeling of his touch, his warm hugs, and passionate kisses.

I had left the door unlocked so that the people from the hospice could let themselves in. When I heard them, I turned around to see two men standing in the doorway, ready to transport Bruce. As soon as I saw one of them, a great sense of peace came over me.

"You're from the Philippines, aren't you?" I asked him.

"Yes," he replied, surprised.

Through my tears, I said, "So is he, and you are here to take him home." It was as if Bruce's life had come full circle, and he was going to a better place, a place that knew no suffering.

As they prepared to move Bruce, the Filipino man stopped and said to me, "He was loved, wasn't he?"

"Yes, very much. Why do you ask?"

"I have been doing this for many years, and I can tell by the expression on his face that he died peacefully. I don't see that very often."

As they wheeled Bruce out, I followed them. Before they placed him in the van, I asked to see him once more. I gave him what would be our last kiss. As I held him, I knew I had fulfilled my promise to be there until the end.

What more can we ask for than to leave this earth loved?

CHAPTER SEVENTEEN

After Bruce died, I cried until there were no more tears left to fall. I began to question if there was truly a God—and if there was, how He could take the man I loved more than anything. And how could He take Bruce's life from him?

Every phone call and text I received was a reminder that Bruce was gone. I got to a point where I believed that if I ignored them, his death wouldn't be real. I wanted to just scream and pick up everything that was in my path and throw it in rage at the unfairness of what had happened. "What did he ever do to deserve such a horrible disease?" I cried.

I had been given a life I never wanted or asked for, and now I was going to have to live it without him. I couldn't imagine how. Bruce was undoubtedly my soul mate, the only man I was ever supposed to love, and now he was gone.

Life had thrown me many challenges in the past. As I conquered each one, I could remind myself that I still had so much life to live, which made me feel that I could continue on. But when Bruce died, life no longer had the same meaning for me. Living without him, I found the days just turned into nights, and as I looked through the darkness, everything seemed pointless.

In the past, my heart had been sad for people who had lost their spouse, but I wasn't able to truly understand the loss they were feeling until the day Bruce died. Suddenly I understood the "brain fog" and helplessness they had described. I had felt a deep sadness after my little brother died, but nothing like this. This was a pain I had no idea how to handle.

I lay on the grass in the backyard, looking up at the sky and clouds, wondering if Bruce was okay and whether his spirit would always be with me. I asked him over and over again to please come home. The night he died, and the following day, I kept saying, "I just want to know you are okay." When I was caring for him at home, I knew he was safe and loved. Where he was now, was he still feeling safe and loved?

Bruce had died on a Friday, and it was on Saturday night that I had my first dream of him. I saw him clearly, as if he were standing before me: his hair was longer and curly, and he was wearing a gray-and-black plaid flannel shirt and black jeans, just like what he wore around the time I first met him. He stood there with a blank stare, waving his hand in a wide arc, from one side of his body to the other. When I woke, I knew he was telling me not to come, but I also felt that he had some deeper message that I wasn't grasping. "You are going to have to give me more than that," I said to him, aloud. "I don't understand."

The answer came about a week later, when I had another dream—a beautiful one this time. I was standing at the door of our house in Hawaii. It opened, and there stood Bruce. This time, his hair was short, and he looked the way he did just before he was diagnosed. He invited me in, gave me a big hug and kiss, and led me to a long white hallway with windows on one side. He turned me around to show me the view. It was the most beautiful, sunny day. The house was perched high above the ocean, and I gazed down at the water. It was brilliant cobalt blue, just like the water on the other side of the island, which he loved.

Bruce grabbed my hand, we walked a few feet, and he stopped and gave me another hug and kiss. He did this two more times, as if he were showing me that he was in a beautiful place and that he missed me. The dream ended as he was kissing me, and when I woke, I had a sense of calm. I knew he was in a place of peace and that I would be there with him one day. In the months that followed, I would have more dreams of him, and they would help to make my grieving a bit easier, because I knew he was watching over me and comforting me.

Right before Bruce died, I had arranged all of the paperwork for his cremation. It hadn't seemed real at the time; and even now, my mind was struggling to accept that it had really happened. Not long after he died, the crematory called me to say he was ready to be picked up. The drive there was surreal. When I arrived, I was greeted by kind staff who were respectful of what I was going through. One of them went upstairs to collect Bruce's ashes, and as I waited, I looked around and wondered: could I do the job they do? Then it occurred to me that, no matter how hard such a job must be at times, these people had also been given a gift: they had the honor of being the last people on earth to touch and hold those who meant everything to their loved ones. I was deeply appreciative of the kindness and respect they showed. The man came back into the room and handed me a plastic box containing Bruce's ashes, and I was glad to have him back with me again, where he belonged.

When I got back home, I lay the container on Bruce's side of the bed, and that is where he rested for a few days. Then I felt it was okay to move him to the nightstand on my side of the bed. That was when I understood that grieving was going to be a matter of making a slow transition. Grief was a long journey, and I had to figure it out for myself, because there was no manual and no way of getting through it quickly. I would have to let things happen when I was ready; there was no set timetable.

All around the house there were reminders of Bruce's journey through cancer. The oxygen machine, the medications near the bed, and the stained sheets that I slept on for days because I didn't want to forget what he had gone through. I had a hard time changing them, because I felt a deep sense of guilt, as if it would mean I were moving on without him. Even after I had changed the bed, for a week I clung to the stained sheets when I slept, as if somehow he was attached to them.

During Bruce's last weeks on earth, Christine, my father's former assistant, with whom I had remained close ever since I'd been a child, had spoken to me every day on the phone. She was my anchor during the hardest time of my life, helping me to find the strength to be able to watch Bruce die. And now that he had gone, I wouldn't have been able to survive without her. She would listen to me ramble on as I fell apart, and after I hung up the phone, I always seemed to feel better. Finally, one day when we were talking, she told me to throw the sheets away. "This isn't how you want to remember him," she said.

Christine was right. She stayed on the phone with me as I walked to the trash. Even though I knew I was doing the right thing, a part of me wanted to delve back into the trash to retrieve the sheets as soon as I'd put them in. Instead, I walked into the house and started putting together all of the unused medical supplies so I could donate them. I experienced a feeling of sadness and relief when the company came to pick up the medical equipment. Slowly the house was changing, and it was starting to hit me just how real it all was and that he had really died.

It was weeks before I could be alone in the guest house, which Bruce had used as an office and his retreat to watch movies. One late afternoon, I went back there to retrieve some bills, and I found myself sitting on the floor in the spot where he had first gone down in a seizure—the place where his cancer journey began. It was as if I were being drawn to that spot to be reminded that he was no longer suffering and was in a better place. I lay there crying and speaking to him, wondering if he knew how much I missed him, how much I loved him, telling him I would be with him one day and to please wait for me and not to meet anyone new. If he heard me in heaven, I knew that what I had said would bring a smile to his face, and he would be telling me that I didn't have to worry, that he would wait for me.

A few minutes later, I found a penny under his chair. The date on it was 1996, the year we met. Someone once told me a story about "pennies from heaven": when you find a penny, it means that someone who died was thinking of you; the date represents a memory or a significant time you shared. After that, some days I would go back to the guest house just to sit in Bruce's chair and remember all the times I had seen him sitting there for hours working on emails and touching up photos.

About a month after Bruce died, I was finally able to force myself to do laundry and put his clothes away. As I opened one of his drawers, I stumbled upon a stack of greeting cards that had been banded and placed on top of his clothing. A note attached read "Melissa, I love you."

As I thumbed through the cards, I realized that he had purchased more than two years' worth of cards for me for every holiday, and a few thank-you cards. It was as if he were saying, "I can't be there to give them to you, but know I am with you." I lost it and grasped the cards to my chest.

Through all of the years we were together, I knew Bruce loved me deeply, but I don't believe I knew just how much until he died and I went back and read the hundreds of cards, notes, and letters he had written me since the day we met. As I read each one, I would fall to the ground in tears, pleading for God to give him back to me, pleading for Bruce to come home.

Most of our friends had no idea what Bruce and I shared in our alone time, because we never felt the need to put it on display. Our life as a couple was our story, not theirs. Now, friends would get teary when I showed them the cards and letters that Bruce had given me while he was alive. "Most people would give anything to have one of these cards, and you have almost a hundred," my friend Giselle said. "I'm so sad your love had to end."

"It doesn't end," I assured her.

Every morning for weeks, I walked into the kitchen and started to prepare Bruce's medication and drink, and then would realize there was no reason to anymore. I had lost a lot of weight in the last two weeks of Bruce's life, because I had no interest in eating, there seemed to be no point in cooking as he wasn't able to eat, and I hadn't slept for eight days. His body was preparing to die, and, frankly, so was a part of me. After he died, my friend Lynn came over to help. I hadn't eaten for days, and, at that point, I didn't care if I ever ate again. She walked me over to a local market, and we picked up a few things. Starting out by drinking Ensure, I began to have an interest in food again. I was thankful for her care, and in a matter of a few weeks I was back to my normal weight.

Still, I wandered through the house with no purpose, in a deep fog, completely lost without Bruce, wondering if I could do this without him. I would open one of his drawers, pull out his favorite clothes, and lie on the ground grasping them, as if I would be able to feel what I had felt while holding him when he wore them.

I lay in bed in the very spot we had created life. When my thoughts went to the place of sorrow in my heart, I would remind myself that this very bed was filled with many years of the love we shared. Making love with him was an experience like none I had ever known before. His touches carried such passion, and with every touch, I could feel the love he had for me. I knew I would never know that kind of love again for as long as I lived.

I was as vulnerable as I had ever felt in my life, trying to make sense of it all, wishing Bruce could be there to hold me so I could feel safe even for just a moment. Friends offered to stay with me, but for some reason I felt I needed to do this by myself, as though if I were on my own, I would find a way to speed up the grieving process and get past the pain. But most days, I would lie in bed numb, as if I were in a dream I couldn't wake from. I no longer knew who I was, and I had no sense of time, nor did I care. I was no longer living, I was existing. I wished that the days would pass quickly, and I would wake and it would be three years later. I had been told that three years was the magic number, when life would become a bit easier.

In California, the weather is perfect most of the year. I would wake to a sunny morning with an empty sickness inside that made it impossible for me to see the beauty of the day. He was gone, so what did I have to live for? How was I going to get through this? At times, I wished God would take me, because I wanted to be with Bruce. But just as I would become comfortable with the idea of leaving this earth, I would be reminded of the pain I saw my parents go through when my little brother died.

Grief is something that I can't really describe. The closest I've come to capturing it is to say that it's "living like you have lost your mind." For the entire first year after Bruce's death, I found myself hatching up ways I could bring him back, as if that were possible. I had always been the problem solver and was efficient at getting things done, so I couldn't conceive that I wasn't able to do this. It was as if I wasn't going to bow down and quit. One minute, I would fall to the ground, engulfed in sadness, pleading for Bruce to come home—and ten minutes later, I would be numb, as if I couldn't feel. I never knew what I would be feeling moment to moment, or day to day, for that matter. The one thing I never did was blame Bruce for leaving—quite the opposite. I was sad he didn't have the choice to stay.

Even though Bruce was gone, I was still able to feel his presence. One day, I went out to sit on the deck to write, and two hummingbirds landed on the branch in the tree right next to me. I remembered his words to me when I asked him how he would communicate with me if anything happened to him: "I can't tell you, but I promise you will know it's me." The tiny birds looked at me and chirped, and I was certain that this was his sign.

Another day, I was walking along the beach with a friend when a little girl walking in front of us began to sing "You Are My Sunshine." It took everything I had to not break apart. Instead, I smiled and took it as a sign from Bruce that he was thinking of me and remembering the times I had sung it to him.

Some people say that when a person passes, they communicate with their loved ones through energy, such as electricity. One night, the air-conditioner came on, out of the blue. My skin began to tingle when I went over to look at it and saw that the switch was set to "Off." In the dining room and TV room, lights would randomly flicker on and off. I called out an electrician, who had no explanation. It went on like this for a month, and then just as suddenly as it had started, it stopped.

I knew Bruce was there, so when I missed him, I would talk to him. "I hope that heaven is beautiful, and that you're up there playing as much tennis and golf as you like," I'd say. When I got together with our friends and remembered and celebrated his life, I would say to him, "I'm not sure if they allow scotch up there, but if so, please enjoy a glass and know that you will never be forgotten."

A month after Bruce passed, I invited more than eighty of his friends to gather in the backyard for his "Celebration of Life." I had spent the whole month organizing it, going from store to store to find everything I needed to make it a beautiful event, because he deserved a truly special day. I woke at 5:00 a.m., surprised to find that it had rained. After only a couple of hours of sleep, I was in a daze as I walked around the backyard, wiping down all the tables and chairs that I'd had delivered, oblivious to how cold it was outside. Just as I finished, the sun came out, and it turned into a beautiful day. I stood on the deck and looked out at what I had created for him, and I knew he would be pleased as he looked down from heaven.

I was still lost in deep grief at this time, and most of the day was a blur to me. I remember the commotion of people chatting and telling stories about Bruce's life. I could hear the sound, but I wasn't able to process the emotions. At one point, I walked into the kitchen and saw that my neighbors had pitched in to help. They were washing dishes and cleaning up, and I appreciated that they cared to make the day a little easier for me.

In the coming year, events would prove that a handful of people I had invited that day hadn't really deserved to be there, even though they were some of Bruce's oldest friends. I know I am not the first person to discover after a loved one's death that some of the people in the deceased's life were driven not by love or friendship but by darker motives. I got a lesson in what greed can drive some people to do, and it would almost cause me to lose faith in humanity. Instead, I learned to walk away from the people who brought me sadness, just as Bruce had done after he was diagnosed. As a friend once said to me, "After someone dies, you find out who your real friends are. The ones that are gone, you will be glad to say goodbye to."

Though it was upsetting to have to deal with the greed of people Bruce had considered close to him, I learned a lot about myself through the experience, and eventually I would find that it had made me a better person. It was a reminder that I should never judge all of humankind based on the actions of just a few people. There will always be terrible people in this world, but maybe they are here to remind the rest of us that we are living our lives right. We have very little control over what others do, and we leave this earth with only one thing: our integrity.

Rather than focusing on those who brought me pain, I found comfort in remembering the love and loyalty that all of the good people in Bruce's life had shown to him before and after his passing.

Another thing that brought me comfort was making lunch for the neuro-oncology doctors who had treated Bruce. As I handed lunch to Dr. Cloughesy, I was greeted with a warmth that always seemed to change my day. I was living in the deepest grief and trying to pretend I was all right. Little did his doctor know just how much his kindness helped me. He gave me faith that I was going to one day be okay.

I would also spend time with the chemotherapy patients. On days when I could see they felt defeated, I would share my story, in hopes they would be inspired to keep fighting to be here. As I left, some would give me a hug, and I knew they were ready to fight again. I went there hoping to make their day a little brighter, but afterward I would feel that they gave me so much more than what I had given them.

I am a very organized person who doesn't procrastinate; I couldn't be late for anything if I tried. But now it took every-thing I had to do the simplest of tasks, like doing laundry and paying bills. There was no motivation for me to get up in the morning, but I did. I forced life to happen. I made plans all day, every day, for months, because an anxiety welled up in me at the idea of being alone. My friends were there for me. Some even changed their family plans just to be with me, and I will never forget all they did for me.

One day, my friend Anita came over, and we sat on the front steps, chatting about where my life would go from here. She said, "Boy, you really have had some bad luck."

"Why do you say that?" I asked.

"All of the things you have gone through!" she said, surprised.

"I never once in my life thought I had bad luck," I said, equally surprised. "If I'd had bad luck, I would have died when I was three months old." I prefer to think of the things that have happened to me as bumps in the road that built my character and made me the person I am today. I have always believed that life is what you make it.

Of course, there were times throughout my life when I questioned why I was I put on this earth to know so much suffering and when the day would come that my life would get easier. After Bruce died, I asked myself that same question again—only this time, I stopped and reminded myself that it was all worth it to have known him and that I was grateful to have survived my medical problems just to have experienced his love.

I had to have the follow-up procedure to see if there were any new growths in my bladder. After I made the appointment, my stomach sank with the realization of how different my life was now. Through all my years of going to doctors' appointments and surgeries, Bruce was always there to take care of me. Who would be there for me if I got sick now? Would I be taken care of with the love and dedication that he'd experienced? With my history of medical issues, these were scary questions. I had never had to ask myself them before, but now I had to face a new reality without Bruce.

I was not one to ask people for help, but I was learning that I didn't have a choice except to reach out to friends. It was a relief to find that so many people stepped up. They helped me realize that I was going to be all right. When I received the test results, which, thankfully, showed that there were no new growths, I could hear Bruce saying to me, "I promised you that you would be okay."

A week later, I flew to our home in Hawaii. As I stepped off the plane, I felt his presence as if he were there, wrapping his arms around me to comfort me. This was the first of many signs I was to receive that would prove he was there with me.

The pain of entering the house was so deep that I fell to the floor in tears, wanting to turn around and head back to the airport. For years, we had followed a routine each time we arrived: I would pull our clothes out of storage bags and wash them so we could wear them during our stay. This time, I wasn't prepared for the emotions that overcame me as I opened the bags.

The house was almost all glass, and as night fell, I was afraid to be there by myself. Again, I asked the question I had already asked a hundred times: "How do I do this without you?" I would always hear Bruce's voice in my head, saying, "You are strong. You can do this. I know it." I spread Bruce's clothes out on the bed and slept on them. They were filled with mildew, but I didn't care. I held them as if he were there. I would sleep on them during my whole stay, and later, I would pack a few pieces of his clothing to take back with me to Los Angeles.

I woke in the darkness of a quiet morning and made my way to the living room, where I lay on a bench by a large window overlooking the ocean, as I had done every morning for eight years when we came to Hawaii. Only now there was a permanent silence, and the home no longer held the joy it once had. I went and sat on the beach and took photos of the sunrise, and as I walked back inside, I was hit with the need to wake Bruce and show him how beautiful it was. But his side of the bed was empty and untouched, and I was left feeling torn and confused being there.

Later that day, I met my friend Tracy for lunch at an old market near the house. As I paid for my lunch, the cashier, who had no idea what I had just gone through, said, "There is a bouquet of flowers outside; I would like for you to have them, on me." As we walked outside and I picked up the flowers, I realized they were the same type that Bruce would buy for me each time we arrived in Hawaii. We looked at each other, and Tracy said, "Can you believe that? You do know that was Bruce."

I had come down with walking pneumonia, and the medication was making me crave sweets. The next morning,

I walked into Whole Foods to buy something to satisfy my craving. As I tried to pay, the cashier said, "This one's on me. Have a nice day!"

The following day, I was feeling a little better and went for a walk on the beach. Everywhere I turned, there were reminders of Bruce and the time we had spent there together. And then, as I turned around to go home, I looked to my right and saw a man standing there. I had to do a double take, because he looked exactly like Bruce. He had the same haircut, was the same height and build, and was wearing a white cutoff t-shirt and black shorts, exactly like the ones Bruce used to wear when I first met him. I hated that t-shirt and used to hide it from him, and he would find it and come out wearing it and laugh. I found myself laughing on the beach. Maybe he was trying to tell me that he was in heaven wearing that t-shirt every day. It reminded me of just how much I missed the way he could make me laugh on the saddest day—and then I realized that even though he was gone, he was still making me laugh. I looked over at the ocean and recalled something a friend had said to me once: "When someone dies, you will see them in a crowd. It's them telling you that they are okay." I had taken my eyes off him for only a moment, and when I looked back, he was gone.

As I watched the sunrise the next morning, I pictured a memory of Bruce in my mind. Every morning, I would wake and look over at him. Most days, he would be sleeping peacefully, with his hand resting on his cheek. I would say to him in a whisper, "I love you." Sometimes he would hear me and reach over to hold me. There was a softness in that moment that I would never forget.

As the days passed, I settled in and began to feel a comfort in being in the house, with all of its memories. I could see Bruce everywhere. This was our home, and we had shared so much here. I found myself looking out across the lawn. I pictured him there playing ball with his son, and, years later, doing the same thing as an old man with his grown son. Once I got past the pain of my memories, I was able to see the beauty of this place that we loved.

When the cab arrived on my last morning in Hawaii, as I closed the front door behind me, I could hear Bruce once again say, "I wish we didn't have to leave." As I made my way to the cab, I stopped and turned around to see what would now be only a bittersweet reminder of a new life that almost happened.

CHAPTER EIGHTEEN

One year after Bruce's death, I would be out with friends, and I'd feel that it might be getting easier. But then I would get home, walk in the door, and again there was that silence. I would once again fall apart, pleading for him to come home. The mornings and evenings were the hardest, when the day was at its most quiet. I would do whatever I could to stay busy to keep my mind off missing him. There were days I would get so sick of keeping busy, but I knew the alternative was worse. I was lost and just wanted to scream out of frustration, "I don't know how to do this! How do I get past this pain?" Every day, I hoped that someone could give me an answer.

It was the hardest year of my life. Every morning I would wake to an empty pillow and be reminded of when we first met and he said, "I know this might sound crazy, but will you move in with me? I want to wake with you every day."

For years, Bruce would tell me, "You need to learn to relax," and I would always say, "I will *relax* when I'm old and I can no longer *do*." It would drive him crazy! About a year after he died, I found that I needed to learn not only how to relax but also how to be alone. It was a confusing time for me, because I hated being alone, and for the first time in my life, I had to figure out how to be. Eventually, I learned how to be okay with solitude and even started to enjoy the peace that came from being alone with my own thoughts. Ironically, Bruce spent almost twenty years trying to help me find quiet, and it was only after his death that I was able to.

One of the ways Bruce relaxed was by reading avidly; it was his form of escape from the everyday. I envied him for being able to sit for hours and read. For most of my life, I was really only interested in reading medical research. I think it came from when I was a child and would have a seizure and forget what I had read; it discouraged me. When Bruce died, I started writing on a daily basis, at times for the entire day, in order to get through the pain of loss. Eventually, this led me to start reading novels, and, like Bruce, I found myself getting lost in the stories. Even though he was gone, he was still teaching me.

I spent my first Christmas and birthday since Bruce's death with my family. When I woke and remembered that he wasn't there to roll over and wish me a Merry Christmas and happy birthday, I felt sad, but I also felt mad, because Bruce didn't have the choice to be there. When I arrived back in Los Angeles, I was faced with the fact that the following day would be my first New Year's Eve without him. I decided to spend it alone, thinking about the year that I had just experienced and setting my intention to begin to heal.

The following day, my friend Laura called to wish me a Happy New Year. Initially, I couldn't see much that was happy about it, but once we got talking and she asked me, "What are you most grateful for this year?" I found, to my own surprise, that my answer was, "Everything."

"Certainly you aren't grateful for the bad stuff," said Laura.

"Actually, I'm grateful even more so for the bad, because the greatest lessons of life and gratitude are born from those moments," I said.

By the time the first anniversary of Bruce's death came around, I was able to make it through half a day before falling apart. This surprised me, when I reflected on how only recently I had been thinking about him and crying constantly throughout the day. It turned out that what people had told me after he died was true. "I promise you—it does get a little easier," they had said. Nothing can prepare you for watching someone you love die, but as each day passed, the pain started to become less piercing, and I began to trust that I would heal and life would begin again. Even though I still felt lost without Bruce, each day there were moments where I thought: Maybe one day I will be okay.

I was ready to fly to Hawaii to scatter Bruce's ashes in the ocean, as he had requested. My friend Agnes came with me to offer her support. We went to sit on the beach, looking out at the ocean, and I heard Bruce express how important it was that his ashes would rest in the place that had brought us so much peace. It was the perfect sunny and warm day. I rented two canoes—one was appropriately named *Ohana Spirit,* which means "family spirit." Agnes and I were taken by the local canoe club to a place where people frequently went to scatter their loved ones' ashes, so that Bruce would have company. I sat there holding his ashes, thinking this still didn't seem real. How could this really be happening? I opened the container and almost started to laugh as I remembered something Bruce had said to me when we talked about his wish to be cremated and have his ashes scattered. He said, "Whatever you do, don't just open the container and try to pour me into the ocean. Pay attention to the wind, because I don't want you to wear me." I forced myself to think sad thoughts so that I wouldn't burst out laughing, because I didn't want people to think I was being disrespectful. We stopped and had a moment of silence, and then I said a prayer for Bruce and spoke to him for a few minutes. After I scattered his ashes, I felt a sense of completion, because I had fulfilled every promise I had ever made to him.

The next day, Agnes and I were flying back to Los Angeles. Bruce and I had a tradition that we would always walk on the beach in the morning one last time before heading to the airport for the 1:00 PM flight. Agnes and I did the same, to honor him. It was a gray morning, and it looked as though we might get rained on during our walk, but as we got back to the house, a break appeared in the clouds, and the sun shone through.

"Look," I said to Agnes, pointing at the ocean. "The sun's shining on the spot where I scattered Bruce's ashes." We looked at each other, amazed. "He's telling me that he is finally home."

☆   ☆   ☆

Life seemed to be getting a little easier. The cloud of intense grief was subsiding, and I had entered the stages of mourning. I thought being around people who understood how I was feeling might help, so I joined a bereavement group. After one of our meetings, I arrived home around 8:30 PM. Coming down the driveway, I noticed that there were lights on in the house. I hadn't left any on. As I opened the back door and walked into the kitchen, I saw that the window had been pushed open. I had this eerie feeling I will never forget, as if the devil had been there. I walked a few steps, and finally it registered that I had been burglarized.

Crying, I walked out the back door and called 911, and in less than five minutes, there were five police cars in front of the house. They had me go next door and stay with the neighbors. When they were sure the house was safe to enter, they came for me and walked me through the house, asking me some questions about what was missing. Things had been thrown everywhere. I couldn't believe the mess the robbers had made in the bedroom. My heart sank when I noticed they had gone through my jewelry box and had stolen every ring Bruce had designed and bought for me over the time we were together. What saddened me the most was that they had taken the rings Bruce had made for me for my birthday when he took me to

Austria just a couple months after we met. Yes, there were more expensive rings that were gone, but those I'd held especially dear.

I had made memory books containing all the cards, letters, and notes Bruce had ever given me since we met. I would be devastated if something had happened to them. The robbers had pulled piles of clothes out of the drawers and strewn them all over the floor, and I began searching under them desperately for the memory books. There they lay on the floor, untouched.

Soon after I'd moved in with Bruce, he'd come back from a working trip to London and presented me with a little wooden box in gift wrapping, with a very special poem attached. I rushed over to the armoire where I kept it and was relieved to see that it was still there.

My eyes welled up with tears, grateful that I still had the things that mattered to me the most—far more than the money and jewelry that had been stolen. The cards and poem that expressed Bruce's love for me would forever be priceless. The other things could be replaced.

I took out the gift-wrapped box and read the poem:

A GIFT OF LOVE
This is a very special gift
That you can never see
The reason it's so special is
It's just for you from me
Whenever you are lonely
Or even feeling blue

You only have to hold this gift
And know I think of you
You never can unwrap it
Please leave the ribbon tied
Just hold this box close to your heart
It's filled with my love inside

I slept at the neighbors', and when I returned the next morning, the house had that same eerie feeling as the night before. I walked into the bedroom, made my way through all the clothes scattered on the floor, sat on the bed, and said out loud, "Who in the hell do you think you are to come into my house and think that my stuff was yours?" I resolved that from that moment on, they were not going to affect me. Their actions were their problem, not mine. They were not going to make me afraid to be in my own home. This latest setback would only make me stronger.

When Bruce and I had first met, I'd given him a memory box in which to store things that were precious to him. It was lying on the floor, discarded by the burglars. I sat down and opened the box for the first time, and discovered that he had kept every card and letter I had given him during our time together. At the bottom was the note I had placed in the box when I gave it to him: "In this box lies your future, and I believe it is filled with love and happiness. Fill it with only good memories so on the sad days you can go to this box to remind you there are many more beautiful memories in store for you."

I had a dream of Bruce that night. He was standing in the bedroom, and it was dimly lit. I was on the floor beside him, holding on to him, as if I were trying to tell him, "Please don't go." I looked up, and he looked into my eyes and said, "I am with you." I woke, and it felt real, as if he were right there with me. Maybe he was.

☆   ☆   ☆

Being adopted was hard for me at times when I was growing up. I didn't know where I fit into this world, and I was left wondering why I was here. What was my purpose? Going through all of my medical crises had also made my life difficult, though somehow I was still able to find beauty in life. I was the girl who wanted everything and wasn't afraid to go after it. To me, fear was just a state of mind, not a reality.

Growing up in a small town across the river from D.C., I had always known I was a city girl. I dreamed of being on the other side of the water, and I knew that one day, no matter what, I would live a city life. It was only when I grew older that I realized I already had everything—and more—than I ever needed to be happy. Spending my early years in that small town helped me understand the simple joys life could bring. My father, a man from the South, lived a life of simplicity. I learned that simplicity from him, and today, I find comfort anywhere I am. It's the love and kindness of people that I thrive on, and it's where I find my peace.

I met Bruce during a time of turmoil after my life-changing brain surgery, and he looked past it and saw only my heart.

He saw the me who had been buried deep down. I learned to embrace my life, and I felt complete for the first time. That was the moment when all that I had gone through turned into a gift. Bruce once said to me, "Reveal the rawness and beauty in your heart, and you will be surprised what will come." He was right.

I had no idea when I met Bruce just how much he would change my life. In our almost twenty years together, we shared more than many people would in ten lifetimes. It hadn't been an easy road for us. Our journey together had taught me that life isn't always easy. Through all of the hard times, something had kept telling me that this was the man I would love more than anyone, and our relationship was worth fighting for.

After he died, his loss brought the strands of my life together; everything about my past and my inner, hidden self made sense. To know the feeling of loving someone deeply, to have the honor of caring for them when they need you the most, to find that you are the one who has been chosen to do it—there is nothing like it. My wish is that everyone can know such love, the kind that shakes the inner core of your soul. I knew when I was taking care of him through his illness that I would never have a more important job in my time here on this earth.

I believe that everything happens for a reason. After all, what were the odds that I would live through so many serious medical problems in order to be there for the man I loved when he had to face the ultimate medical ordeal? Even so, I don't know if I will ever understand why Bruce was taken at the time in his life when he was the happiest. This may sound crazy, but after his death, there were moments when I believed that the reason Bruce had come into my life was to protect and care for me during my years of serious medical problems, and once I was healthy and his job was done, he had to leave. Bruce was 44 when we first met. And what age was I at the time of his death? Forty-four. It was as if he felt he could leave after he had got me to the place where he was when we met. It's amazing where the mind goes when there are no answers to its questions.

Earlier in our relationship, I had believed that it was me who had been sent into Bruce's life to teach him how to trust, how to be vulnerable and accept another's love and care. It was only when he died that I realized he had taught me the same. Until I met him, I always felt that I needed to be the strong one and the caregiver. I thought I didn't need anyone's help, because I could handle everything that life dished up. By caring for me, he allowed me to realize that I didn't always have to be so strong. I learned to trust that he was right there to help me and that I wasn't alone.

In the past, I'd felt our relationship was mostly about me being there for him, when in reality he was there for me in ways I couldn't see until now. It was if, at the end of Bruce's life, I had been given the opportunity to give back in the most profound way.

I learned to love even more deeply than I ever thought was possible. Going through his illness together stripped life down to its absolute raw, pure beauty, its essence. Only then did I truly see the meaning of love and the gift I'd had since the day I met him.

He inspired me every day to be a better person. His love—and death—helped me reveal the greatest version of myself. In his last years, I learned what real gratitude is. I have always had a deep appreciation for the beauty and kindness in the world, but loving and caring for Bruce and watching him die, savoring every single moment of life together, took gratitude to the highest level of the human soul.

Bruce took a piece of my heart with him when he died, so that one day I would be able to find him again. Only I don't believe there is an end. I believe when you love someone deeply, they are with you always. I had always felt that my soul and Bruce's soul had traveled many lifetimes, and that when he died, our journey wasn't over—there was much more to come.

During my husband's medical treatment, I created a website for cancer patients and their caregivers that would hopefully help make their journey easier and kinder.

www.Hope2MD.org

CPSIA information can be obtained
at www.ICGtesting.com
Printed in the USA
LVOW03s2055231217
560697LV00001B/338/P

9 780997 485066